A Gift For

_____

From

_____

Date

_____

the
simple joys
of
Motherhood

Heartwarming Stories & Inspiration to Celebrate Mom

Ellie
Claire
gift & paper expressions

...inspired by life

Ellie Claire™ Gift & Paper Corp.
Minneapolis, MN 55378
EllieClaire.com

The Simple Joys of Motherhood
© 2013 by Ellie Claire Gift & Paper Corp.

ISBN 978-1-60936-785-5

All Scripture quotations, unless otherwise indicated, are taken from The Holy Bible, New International Version® (NIV)®. Copyright © 1973, 1978, 1984, 2011 by Biblica. Used by permission of Zondervan. All rights reserved worldwide. Other Scripture references are from the following sources: The Holy Bible, New Living Translation (NLT) copyright © 1996, 2004, 2007 by Tyndale House Foundation. Used by permission of Tyndale House Publishers Inc., Carol Stream, Illinois 60188. The New American Standard Bible® (NASB), Copyright © 1960, 1962, 1963, 1968, 1971, 1972, 1973, 1975, 1977, 1995 by The Lockman Foundation. Used by permission. *The Message* (MSG) © 1993, 1994, 1995, 1996, 2000, 2001, 2002 by Eugene Peterson. Used by permission of NavPress, Colorado Springs, CO. The Holy Bible, King James Version (KJV). The Holy Bible, New King James Version (NKJV). Copyright © 1997, 1990, 1985, 1983 by Thomas Nelson, Inc. The New Revised Standard Version Bible (NRSV), copyright 1989, 1995, Division of Christian Education of the National Council of the Churches of Christ in the United States of America. Used by permission. The New Century Version® (NCV). Copyright © 1987, 1988, 1991, 2005 by Thomas Nelson, Inc. Used by permission. *The Living Bible* (TLB) © 1971. Used by permission of Tyndale House Publishers, Inc., Carol Stream, Illinois 60188. All rights reserved.

Excluding Scripture verses, references to men and masculine pronouns have been replaced with gender-neutral references.

Compiled by Marilyn Jansen
Cover and interior design by ThinkPen | thinkpen.com
Illustrations by Julie Sawyer Phillips
Typesetting by Jeff Jansen | aestheticsoup.net

Printed in China

Contents

All mothers are rich when they

love their children....

Their love is always

the most beautiful of joys.

MAURICE MAETERLINCK

The Most Beautiful of Joys

Motherhood is rich in simple joys, those little moments of love between a mother and her child that interrupt the mundane and transform it into something amazing.

Simple joys may be found in the delight of catching fireflies in the backyard or the surprise of receiving a birthday package in the mail. They may be the sweetness of a lullaby, the childlike faith of a murmured prayer, the pride of budding independence, or the wholehearted trust of a child coming to you for advice.

Our prayer is that *The Simple Joys of Motherhood* will encourage you to celebrate the little wonders as they come. To embrace the blessing of being a mom. And to recognize that those little "mom moments" you share with your child are the most beautiful of joys.

~The Editors

the simple joy of Togetherness

What will your children remember? Moments spent listening, talking, playing, and sharing together may be the most important times of all.

GLORIA GAITHER

Take your everyday, ordinary life—your sleeping, eating, going-to-work, and walking-around life—and place it before God as an offering. Embracing what God does for you is the best thing you can do for him.

ROMANS 12:1 MSG

Togetherness, the Good Part of Each Day

BY BONNIE JENSEN

All I want is for you to be able to develop a way of life in which you can spend plenty of time together with the Master without a lot of distractions.

1 CORINTHIANS 7:35 MSG

What every child craves is something every parent can give—*togetherness*. We spend so much time worrying about things—from a clean house, to a manicured lawn, to the list of things to do tomorrow that we didn't get done today. With all the distractions, we often lose track of our child's needs.

Yet, there is only one thing needed. It's the good part—the sitting together to make eye contact and to listen. The part where we hear what a child's heart has to say in simple, honest, *I-need-you* words. The moments when they feel alone or neglected…when they're hurting… when they reach for us, and we can show them how God loves. He knows the distractions. He pays attention. He makes us all feel incredibly valuable and loved.

Together time, no matter when or where it happens, is time to heap love on our children and show them they're a God-given good part of our day. It is a way of living that says to a child, "you are priceless."

Nothing can match the treasure of common memories,
of trials endured together, of quarrels
and reconciliations and generous emotions.

ANTOINE DE SAINT-EXUPÉRY

*Friends love through all kinds of weather,
and families stick together in all kinds of trouble.*

PROVERBS 17:17 MSG

Father, help me to take the time
to create stories with my children.
May good memories hold
the generations together. Amen.

SCOTT WALKER

The LORD is good and his love
endures forever; his faithfulness continues
through all generations.

PSALM 100:5

Talking Together

Be happy with those who are happy, and weep with those who weep.
ROMANS 12:15 NLT

I'd been working on my speech for weeks, maybe years. It was the final night at home for our two daughters before they headed off to college. I wanted to remind them to do their best and to choose their friends wisely and not to dillydally away their study time. I needed to make sure they knew how important it was to attend class and to take careful notes.

I summoned them into my bedroom.

"Girls," I began, "there are some things you should remember when you're away at school."

We stood awkwardly in silence for a few moments. Then Katie, the eighteen-year-old, casually stretched out on the floor to hear my lengthy instructions. She's always been the jokester. Twenty-year-old Jamie plopped down next to her, put her hands behind her head, and stared at the ceiling fan.

"Let's just talk, Mom. Like we used to," Katie suggested.

"Yeah, that'd be neat," Jamie agreed.

Skip the speech? But do they know enough? Are they ready? I wondered.

Then we did something we'd never done before: I joined them on the floor, and the three of us, our feet touching one another's heads, formed a triangle. We talked and laughed about everything from the funny things that had happened during their childhoods to what color toenail polish looked the best and whose Barbie dolls had been dressed the finest.

As we said good night, I smiled from way down deep. Laughter would always hold us together. The rest, I'd leave up to God.

Talking into the night, singing songs in the car, holding hands through scary situations—
these times spent together are the bright points of joy in a mother's day. They spur laughter, closeness, and understanding. They make our children—and us—
feel loved and comforted.

MARILYN JANSEN

According to research, kids say it's the simple things—like taking walks, sharing meals, playing games, watching TV, and just talking—
that they want more of with their parents.

You're not in this alone. I want you woven into a tapestry of love, in touch with everything there is to know of God.

COLOSSIANS 2:1–2 MSG

TWENTY ACTIVITIES TO ENCOURAGE TOGETHERNESS

1. Walk or bike or snowshoe to the park.
2. Have a family movie marathon night.
3. Attend a music concert together.
4. Visit a zoo and give the animals names.
5. Make a lemonade stand.
6. Plant a vegetable or flower garden or trees.
7. Visit all local shops together, especially the quirky ones.
8. Have a watermelon seed–spitting contest.
9. Check out books from the library and read to each other.
10. Make funny narration while watching family videos or going through photo albums.
11. Take a road trip—turn off the personal electronic devices.
12. Learn Morse code or sign language together.
13. Play a card or board game.
14. Camp out or build a snow fort in the backyard.
15. Cook a meal together.
16. Visit a nursing home or elderly person.
17. Do a scavenger hunt at a museum.
18. Play a round of miniature golf.
19. Do chores to music.
20. Roast marshmallows over a campfire or in the fireplace.

Sticking Together

So wherever I am there's always Pooh,
There's always Pooh and Me.
"What would I do?" I said to Pooh,
"If it wasn't for you," and Pooh said: "True,
It isn't much fun for One, but Two
Can stick together," says Pooh, says he.
"That's how it is," says Pooh.

A. A. MILNE

Together we stick; divided we're stuck.

EVON HEDLY

There is a friend who sticks closer than a brother.

PROVERBS 18:24

[Do not] forget the obvious, the little joys, the meals together, the
birthday celebrations, the weeping together in time of pain, the wonder
of the sunset, or the daffodil peeping through the snow.

MADELEINE L'ENGLE

Clothe yourselves with tenderhearted mercy, kindness, humility,
gentleness, and patience. Make allowance for each other's faults, and
forgive anyone who offends you…. Above all, clothe yourselves with love,
which binds us all together in perfect harmony.

COLOSSIANS 3:12–14 NLT

9

Stitched Together

BY KATHY MORRISON

Father to the fatherless, defender of widows—
this is God, whose dwelling is holy.
God places the lonely in families…and gives them joy.

PSALM 68:5–6 NLT

I heard the front door open, then voices and laughter. I threw myself on my bed. My new stepfather's sisters had come down from Chicago to visit us in Alabama for the week. I wanted no part of them. "They can't wait to get to know you," Mom had said. But I didn't want to get to know them. It had been hard enough accepting a stepfather. Now I'd have to accept this other family too? I was a ball of anxiety, so I decided to pray. *Lord, make these people go away!*

Mom was calling, "Kathy, come down, please!" I put on a fake smile and dragged myself into the living room. I stopped, surprised. My stepfather's sisters weren't just talking, they were knitting. "Sit next to your aunt Kay and your aunt Mary Lou," Mom said. I did as she asked, still staring at the aunts' knitting. They asked me questions in their funny northern accent, about school, about what I was interested in. I answered reluctantly. But I couldn't tear my eyes away from what they were doing. They dodged the needles in and out, creating a colorful pattern almost without looking. It was so cool!

They must have noticed me staring. "Wanna try?" asked Aunt Kay.

"Here," said Aunt Mary Lou. "How about this color?" She handed me some light blue yarn and a pair of knitting needles.

"I—I don't know how," I stammered.

"We'll show you," Aunt Kay said. "First you have to cast on…."

I watched as she guided the needles in and out. Might as well give it a try. "That's it," the aunts encouraged. I started to get the hang of it. After an hour I had…something. A square. Aunt Mary Lou generously christened it a pot holder. The stitches were loose and I had lost a few. But my new aunts just beamed. "Keep trying," Aunt Kay said.

All week they worked with me. And I opened up. "What did you do today?" my stepfather asked Wednesday evening. Instead of ignoring him, I said, "Check this out," and showed him a scarf I'd made. He looked surprised—and proud. By the end of the week, I didn't want my aunts to leave. They gave me patterns for hats and scarves and even let me keep a pair of needles and my choice of yarn. Maybe my stepfather and his family weren't so terrible after all. On another visit, I learned how my aunts got started. "Our family came from Yugoslavia to Wisconsin, and we were very poor," Aunt Kay said. Her mom knit "sockies" to keep their feet warm, an art she'd learned from her mother in the old country. Knitting was a family tradition, passed down from generation to generation. Now it had passed on to me. I'm a part of this family, and my stepfather, my aunts, are all part of mine.

Sixteen years later, I'm still knitting. God *didn't* answer my prayer to make my aunts go away. Instead, He used them to show me that my new stepfather and his family could be stitched together with my own.

Family Togetherness

Children just don't fit into a to-do list very well. It takes time
to be an effective parent when children are small.
It takes time to introduce them to good books. It takes time
to fly kites and play ball and put together
jigsaw puzzles. It takes time to listen.

DR. JAMES DOBSON

Regarding life together and getting along with each other…
you're God-taught in these matters. Just love one another!

1 THESSALONIANS 4:9 MSG

How many hopes and fears, how many ardent wishes and
anxious apprehensions are twisted together in the threads
that connect the parent with the child!

SAMUEL GRISWOLD GOODRICH

How sweet the sound of laughing together, of sharing the joy
of knowing each other so well.

Stay on good terms with each other, held together by love.
HEBREWS 13:1 MSG

To live in prayer together is to walk in love together.
MARGARET MOORE JACOBS

Make my joy complete by being like-minded, having the same love,
being one in spirit and of one mind.
PHILIPPIANS 2:2

Snowflakes are one of nature's most fragile things,
but just look what they can do when they stick together.
VESTA M. KELLY

Love puts the fun in together...
the sad in apart...
the hope in tomorrow...
the joy in a heart.

A Togetherness Table

BY CAROL KUYKENDALL

Let us love one another, for love comes from God.

1 JOHN 4:7

I want a user-friendly, sturdy table that people are drawn to, not only to eat but to read the newspaper or have a cup of coffee or play games. I call it a family table because it's the kind of place where "family" happens.

The family table of my childhood was an oblong glass table that my mother had inherited from an aunt. My mother insisted it set a proper tone for our family with four rambunctious children. It was the only place where we came together regularly.

Then there was the family table my husband and I had when our children were growing up—a heavy wooden trestle table with a bench along one side so we could add people without scouring the house for chairs. Our photo albums show what happened around that table: birthday parties, pumpkin carvings, Valentine's Day dinners, science projects. Love.

Now I want a family table with comfortable chairs that beckon both adults and children. I may not get my dream table for a while, so in the meantime I'm taking note of what else beckons and connects people, like our big comfy couch in front of the fireplace, a bunch of stools pulled up to the kitchen counter, and, most of all, the presence of God in the words and attitudes of the people who live in our home.

A single conversation across the table with
a wise person is worth a month's study of books.

CHINESE PROVERB

The incredible gift of the ordinary!
Glory comes streaming from the table of daily life.

MACRINA WIEDERKEHR

Sixty percent of teens say they have dinners with their families at least five times a week. This has remained consistent over the past decade. During those dinners, 75 percent say they talk to their parents about what's going on, and 72 percent say that eating dinner frequently with their parents is very or fairly important.

CENTER ON ADDICTION AND SUBSTANCE ABUSE

Bound Together

BY BRIGITTE WEEKS

God, we thank you; we thank you because you are near.
We tell about the miracles you do.

PSALM 75:1 NCV

We took an unruly crew of ten on a two-week vacation to a large house in the Loire Valley of France.

Everyone got along just fine—except in the kitchen. He wanted to cook spaghetti; she wanted a vegetarian menu. Her two-year-old wasn't allowed any refined sugar; a three-year-old announced he would only eat peanut butter....

When it was all over, 1,300 quite wonderful digital pictures showed up in my e-mail from four camera-happy parents. The challenge felt daunting, but I clicked and dragged, deleted and pasted through 272 pictures. One final click and they were turned into a lovely book. A few days later, five copies arrived via "snail mail."

I've always believed in miracles—that there were, indeed, enough loaves and fishes for the five thousand, and that water turned into wine at the wedding in Cana. But we aren't used to witnessing miracles in the twenty-first century. As I turned the brightly colored pages, I realized that the miracle in these pictures was timeless: the love and laughter that binds a family together.

CHAPTER 2

The simple joy of Prayer

If we want our children to pray, they must hear us pray. There is no greater demonstration of God's power to our children than when they see their own parents receive answers to prayer.

QUIN SHERRER

I call on you, O God, for you will answer me;
turn your ear to me and hear my prayer.
Show me the wonders of your great love.

PSALM 17:6–7

The Lifeline of Prayer

BY BONNIE JENSEN

Evening and morning and at noon I will pray...and He shall hear my voice.
PSALM 55:17 NKJV

*T*here's nothing more beautiful than easy conversation—the kind that happens between hearts that are completely comfortable with one another. Talking to God can be like that. Teaching our children to pray is revealing to them that God is approachable and loving, kind and forgiving, attentive and active in our lives. He never turns a deaf ear, nor is He ever distracted from the voice of our thankfulness, the expression of our joy, the cry of our pain, or the petition of our needs.

Prayer is the combination of power and privilege. Through the *power of the promise* of His Word, we have *the privilege* to go to God at any time for any reason and know that He's listening and that He'll answer us. Once our children follow our example, a wonderful thing transpires. Their hearts are incredibly open and honest, so fresh from the hands that knit them together that *they* begin to teach *us*.

God is every child's lifeline to strength, hope, peace, confidence, security, joy, and love—and we help them grab onto it by simply praying *for* them and *with* them.

The Gift of Children

Heavenly Father, my prayer to You today is one of thanks-giving, gratitude, and praise. Thank You so much for Your favor and marvelous generosity to my family and me. Every good and perfect gift truly comes directly from Your hand to us through Your giving heart of kindness and love.

I cannot begin to express to You how greatly blessed and grateful I am for the gift of my children. I do, with all my heart, receive each life that has come into our family as Your beautiful gift. I cannot find the words to thank You enough.

ROY LESSIN

Every good and perfect gift is from above,
coming down from the Father of the heavenly lights,
who does not change like shifting shadows.

JAMES 1:17

Words to Grow On

BY DEE WALLACE STONE

By day the LORD directs his love, at night his song is with me—
a prayer to the God of my life.

PSALM 42:8

As an actress, I've often played mothers. I was the mother in several films, including *E.T.* and *Cujo*, and on TV in *The New Lassie* series and, most recently, *The Office*. In November 1988, after years of waiting, my husband, Chris, and I had a baby daughter, Gabrielle. Right from the beginning we decided that we would see to it that Gabrielle was brought up in a positive atmosphere, that whenever we could, we would affirm those qualities we hoped she'd take with her into adulthood. We prayed that she'd be happy, healthy, and balanced, with a good sense of self-esteem.

Psychologists say the most impressionable time in a child's day is the half hour before bedtime. So with Gabrielle, we used this period to read books together and sing to her. Often we would sing a lullaby that a friend wrote for her. And always the last thing we did was sing the prayer my parents used to sing to me—a variation on a familiar bedtime prayer:

Now I lay me down to sleep,
Angels guarding over me,
Like the birdies in the trees,
Heavenly Father, care for me.

The prayer always ended with requests that God bless Mommy and Daddy and grandparents and playmates, and yes, our dogs too.

But each night as Gabrielle went to bed, there was one blessing that we hoped she would take with her as she drifted off to sleep. We would tell her that Mommy loved her and Daddy loved her, but above all we affirmed these three simple, most powerful words to grow on: *God loves you.*

Prayer isn't about words…. It's about trust—trust that God understands what we need and how we feel.

MARIA MASSEI-ROSATO

I love the LORD because he hears my voice
and my prayer for mercy.
Because he bends down to listen,
I will pray as long as I have breath!

PSALM 116:1–2 NLT

PRAYER OF A YOUNG CHILD

*Bless my mommy
and daddy…
and dear God,
take good care
of Yourself.
If anything
happens to You,
we're sunk.*

SIMPLE GRATITUDE PRAYER

Thank You for the world so sweet,
Thank You for the food we eat,
Thank You for the birds that sing,
Thank You, God, for everything.
Amen.

THE LORD'S PRAYER

Our Father who is in heaven, hallowed be Your name.
Your kingdom come. Your will be done, on earth as it is in heaven.
Give us this day our daily bread.
And forgive us our debts, as we also have forgiven our debtors.
And do not lead us into temptation, but deliver us from evil.
For Yours is the kingdom and the power and the glory forever. Amen.

MATTHEW 6:9–13 NASB

It Is All in the Perspective

Dear God,
Did You really mean, "Do unto others as
they do unto you"? If You did, then I'm
going to get even with my brother.

JACKIE

Dear God,
Help my children to love each other with
compassion and understanding. Help them to learn
patience and forgiveness. Fill their hearts with
mercy for each other. And if that isn't
possible right now, help them to fall asleep quickly
before they can concoct a sneaky retaliation plot.

JACKIE'S MOM

Do to others as you would like them to do to you.

LUKE 6:31 NLT

The Sweetest Words

BY ERIN KEELEY MARSHALL

Hallelujah! Praise GOD from heaven,
praise Him from the mountaintops; Praise Him!

PSALM 148:1 MSG

A child's prayers have to be some of the sweetest words ever spoken. There are two reasons I love my daughter's prayers: First, they come straight from her heart—whatever is topmost in her thoughts—and second, they're all about giving thanks.

She's typically eager to pray, and she usually says something like this: "Tanks You, Jesus, for pink fire trucks and for Daddy and Mama and Paxton-boy. And tanks You, Jesus, for doggies and yogurt and mine cozy bed. Amen—Go get it!"

I adore the "Go get it!" she adds to the end. We have no idea where she heard it; she said it came from her head. Knowing her, it probably did. Anyway, because her prayers are loaded with thanksgiving instead of requests, the "Go get it!" isn't a demand that Jesus do her beckoning. It's more like she's cheering Him on and praising Him: "You go, Jesus! You're the best!"

My children inspire me to be simple before Jesus, to praise Him with my first thoughts, to cheer Him on for being Him—for being my victorious Savior, attentive Friend, holy Lord, and mighty King.

*The God who made your children will
hear your petitions. He has promised to do so.
After all, He loves them more than you do.*

MAX LUCADO

If you...know how to give good gifts to your children,
how much more will your heavenly Father
give the Holy Spirit to those who ask him.

LUKE 11:13 NLT

More things are wrought by prayer
Than this world dreams of.

ALFRED, LORD TENNYSON

In my desperation I prayed, and the LORD listened;
he saved me from all my troubles.

PSALM 34:6 NLT

Pray Always

BY PATTI PHILLIPS

Don't worry about anything; instead, pray about everything.
Tell God what you need, and thank him for all he has done.

PHILIPPIANS 4:6 NLT

The thought of facing a night without a doctor's diagnosis and proper medication for my sick daughter finally outweighed my fear of driving on the icy, snowbanked streets. I tucked her under a blanket on the backseat, and while the engine warmed, I bowed my head and asked God to give us protection. We made our way in complete safety.

Several days later when the illness and storm were long past, we again got into the car. This time without a moment's hesitation, I warmed the engine and backed out into the street.

"Aren't we going to pray this time, Mama?" a little voice asked.

She caught me off guard. Instinctively, I turn to God when worried or fearful. But when the crisis is over, how human it is to forget to include Him in the good times.

"Yes," I said to my daughter. "We *are* going to pray."

There is no pretense in simple prayer. We do not pretend to be more holy, more pure, or more saintly than we actually are.... And in this posture, we pour out our heart to the God who is greater than our heart and who knows all things.

RICHARD FOSTER

God has surely listened and has heard my prayer.
Praise be to God, who has not rejected my prayer
or withheld his love from me!

PSALM 66:19–20

As parents, we have a lot to pray about. Praying for our children is one of our greatest parental responsibilities. What an awesome thought to know that God hears and answers our prayers!

KIM BOYCE

A mother's love is like a beacon
Burning bright with faith and prayer
And through the changing scenes of life
We can find a haven there.

HELEN STEINER RICE

A Birthday Wish

BY KAREN BARNETT

Be joyful in hope, patient in affliction, faithful in prayer.
ROMANS 12:12

Andrew, my four-year-old, knelt by his bed.

"Dear God, thank You for this day and please don't let me have any nightmares," he said. "And please let my friend Eden come to my birthday party."

"Sweetie, Eden's new house is hundreds of miles away," I said, pulling the covers over Andrew and kissing his forehead. "That's much too far to come to your party."

"But, Mom," Andrew said, looking at me as if I just didn't understand how life worked, "I prayed she would come!"

I was the last person on earth to tell anyone about prayer. I kept my own prayers strictly on the safe side. Nothing big. Nothing extraordinary.

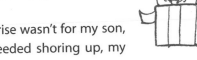

Let the kids have a good day. Keep us safe in the car. Help the baby stop crying. I figured if I kept my expectations low, I wouldn't be disappointed.

Andrew had no such rules. He couldn't imagine turning five without his best friend. I had shown Andrew on a map just how far away Eden lived.

He handed me an invitation with her name on it. I slipped it into my purse. There was no point in mailing it.

"What kind of cake should I make for Saturday?" I asked, hoping to get him thinking about things that were actually possible.

"A purple butterfly," said Andrew. "Eden loves butterflies—and purple is her favorite color."

Thursday evening, the phone rang. It was Eden's mother. "Eden and I are in town this weekend. We'd like to stop by. Are you busy on Saturday?"

I couldn't wait to surprise Andrew. When Eden showed up on Saturday right on time for the party, I grabbed my camera to get a shot of Andrew's face. But Andrew wasn't surprised at all! He welcomed her just like he did his other friends. Then they both ran to play games.

That's when I realized the surprise wasn't for my son, but for me. It was my faith that needed shoring up, my prayers that needed to grow.

"Wasn't it amazing that Eden came all that way to be at your party?" I asked Andrew later.

Andrew looked at me and grinned. "Mom, I prayed!"

A mother who prays is a woman after God's heart, for the children He puts in her care are what His kingdom is made of—"Let the little children come to Me, and do not forbid them; for of such is the kingdom of heaven" (Matthew 19:14 NKJV). Such pure hearts need only simple direction. When we pray, our children learn they are welcome in God's presence, and they become confident in going to Him. As praying mothers, we not only *let* our children come to Him, we *lead* them to Him for life.

BONNIE JENSEN

Prayer should be the key of the day and the lock of the night.

THOMAS FULLER

And now…being the God you are…, please, just one more thing: Bless my family; keep your eye on them always. You've already as much as said that you would, Master GOD! Oh, may your blessing be on my family permanently!

2 SAMUEL 7:28–29 MSG

CHAPTER 3

The simple joy of a Celebration

We are the celebrants out dancing in a
wild rain of grace.... When we lay the soil of
our hard lives open to the rain of grace and let
joy penetrate our cracked and dry places...*life* grows.

ANN VOSKAMP

This is the day the LORD has made;
We will rejoice and be glad in it.

PSALM 118:24 NKJV

Celebrating the Joy

BY BONNIE JENSEN

They celebrate your abundant goodness
and joyfully sing of your righteousness.

PSALM 145:7

*E*very day we're given on this earth is special. No matter what, and no matter what happened yesterday, today is a day to celebrate because God is good and He's *good to us*—all of the time. Shouldn't we teach our children that? Teach them the significance of a sunrise and of the mercy, grace, hope, and the brand-new slate that comes with each morning?

When we choose joy, we choose God. We allow Him to be the One to set our days ablaze with a celebratory spirit that cannot be quenched by circumstance or trial. We set the tone for our days and for our children's days as well. The "joy effect" is truly amazing—it can embolden them to see things with a positive attitude and change the world around them.

Each day is a gift. The days come together to make the pieces of our God-created lives a beautiful whole. Celebrating life is celebrating God.

The grace of God means something like: Here is your life. You might never have been, but you are because the party wouldn't have been complete without you. Here is the world. Beautiful and terrible things will happen. Don't be afraid. I am with you. Nothing can ever separate us. It's for you I created the universe. I love you.

FREDERICK BUECHNER

Celebrate God all day, every day.
I mean, revel in him!

PHILIPPIANS 4:4 MSG

What will your children remember? There is something in every season, in every day, to celebrate with thanksgiving.

GLORIA GAITHER

To everything there is a season,
A time for every purpose under heaven.

ECCLESIASTES 3:1 NKJV

Celebration is more than a happy feeling.
Celebration is an experience.
It is liking others, accepting others, laughing with others.

DOUGLAS R. STUVA

Remember to Celebrate

BY JULIE GARMON

Whoever regards one day as special does so to the Lord.

ROMANS 14:6

Thomas, our youngest, had forgotten my birthday. It was so unlike him. He was not quite sixteen when I turned forty-seven. Sure, he'd said "Happy birthday," but there was no homemade card or even a hug. Maybe he was too busy for his old mom.

On the day after my birthday, I woke up and lay in bed for a few minutes, remembering the births of our children. My mind moved on to the difficult teenage years of our two daughters, now in their twenties. *Thomas's time is coming*, I thought. *How will I deal with that? His rebellion has probably started. See, I'm not important to him anymore.*

Minutes later I heard, "Mom, can you come here?" I slid into my slippers and plodded to the kitchen. Thomas had gotten up early, clipped roses from the yard, put them in a vase, toasted and buttered a bagel just the way I like it, and poured my orange juice. He even put out strawberry jelly and a spoon.

"Happy birthday, Mom. Sorry I forgot yesterday." He'd passed me in height over the last year, but he still gave me one of his best little-boy hugs.

"You're going to make a mighty fine husband," I said.

Then I glanced out the open window and spotted the wild dogwood in full bloom. I heard the birds singing. They'd been at it since daybreak, but somehow I'd missed them.

The holidays are welcome to me partly because
they are such rallying points for the affections,
which get so much thrust aside in the business
and preoccupations of daily life.

GEORGE E. WOODBERRY

What happens when we live God's way?
He brings gifts into our lives…
things like affection for others,
exuberance about life, serenity.

GALATIANS 5:22 MSG

A Celebration of Memories

Sooner or later, we all discover that the important moments in life are not the advertised ones, not the birthdays, the graduations, the weddings, not the great goals achieved. The real milestones are less prepossessing. They come to the door of memory.

SUSAN B. ANTHONY

Today's bright moments are tomorrow's fond memories.

I've thrown myself headlong into your arms—I'm celebrating…. I'm singing at the top of my lungs, I'm so full of answered prayers.

PSALM 13:5–6 MSG

There is nothing higher and stronger and more wholesome and useful for life in later years than some good memory, especially a memory connected with childhood, with home. If a person carries many such memories with them into life, they are safe to the end of their days, and if we have only one good memory left in our hearts, even that may sometime be the means of saving us.

FYODOR DOSTOYEVSKY

Memories are perhaps the best gifts of all.

GLORIA GAITHER

The happiness of life is made up of little things—
a smile, a hug, a moment of shared laughter.

Yes, we should make the most of what God gives, both the bounty and
the capacity to enjoy it, accepting what's given and delighting in the
work. It's God's gift! God deals out joy in the present, the now.

ECCLESIASTES 5:18–19 MSG

If we celebrate the years behind us, they become stepping-stones
of strength and joy for the years ahead.

Satisfy us in the morning with your unfailing love,
that we may sing for joy and be glad all our days.

PSALM 90:14

A Reason to Party

BY MARY LOU CARNEY

Where two or three gather in my name, there am I with them.
MATTHEW 18:20

I often make big dinners for my extended family. We began calling these events "parties" for the little ones. "Nina, are we having a party tonight?" my grandson Drake would ask if I stopped by his house. And his little brother Brock would join in: "Party! Party!" Not long ago, I bought a little neon light. It spells out the word "party" in a rainbow of colors. Once everyone has arrived for dinner, the grandchildren gather round while I plug it in.

Last night my daughter Amy Jo called to see if I could take care of the boys for the evening. Drake and Brock and I dined alone on spaghetti and meatballs that I'd pulled out of the freezer. As we settled down at the table, Drake suddenly sat up and pointed. "The party light, Nina. We forgot the party light!"

"But it's just the three of us," I began.

Drake smiled. "But it's still a party!"

So I plugged in the light. And in the autumn twilight, it glowed soft and inviting. We ate in silence, the only sound was the slurping of spaghetti into small mouths. I think I sense God's presence most during these simple times, times when I find myself standing in a small oasis of gratitude. There I recognize how blessed I am, that I—and those I love— are not alone on this earthly trek.

How much of our lives are...well...so daily. How often our hours are filled with the mundane, seemingly unimportant things that have to be done, whether at home or work. These very "daily" tasks could become a celebration of praise. "It is through consecration," someone has said, "that drudgery is made divine."

GIGI GRAHAM TCHIVIDJIAN

You'll welcome us with open arms when we run for cover to you. Let the party last all night! Stand guard over our celebration.

PSALM 5:11 MSG

There is always something to be joyous about. Always something to celebrate. Another birthday is only one of them.

FRANCIS NAFF

We should look for reasons to celebrate—an A on a paper—even a good hair day!

PAM FARREL

*A*s mothers, we tend to the details, routines, and rhythms of our homes. Traditions, whether they be simple or grand, let our families know the importance of being connected to one another. They become something to look forward to, building a sense of security in our children that they'll want to pass on. When we carry them out, we put value on what is most important—time spent together, celebrating who we are.

BONNIE JENSEN

CELEBRATE FAMILY BY STARTING A FEW TRADITIONS

1. Have a birthday hat for the birthday person to wear during dinner. Decorate an old hat yourself or purchase one that works for your family and reuse it for each birthday.
2. Celebrate the first day of spring by planting your favorite vegetable or flower seeds in a pot. Place it near a window until it can be transplanted or taken outside for the season.
3. Pick one Saturday a month to have a big noisy breakfast with the whole family. Include Grandma's special recipe, your aunt's serving dish, or other things that rekindle family stories and memories.
4. Fill small Easter baskets with food, candy, and the resurrection story to distribute to shelters or senior living centers on Good Friday.

5. Have a squirt gun battle on Independence Day. Whether the battle is held in your backyard, in a local park, or by the seashore, the water will keep everyone cool in the summer heat.

6. Over Labor Day weekend, take a day to "labor for a neighbor." Do yard work, housework, handyman chores, or errand running for people who cannot do it themselves. Then celebrate by taking the family out for ice cream.

7. Have an autumn bonfire once a year. Roast hot dogs and marshmallows or serve cider and pumpkin bread. Pile leaves as high as possible and let the kids jump in.

8. Start a Christmas treat exchange among family members or neighbors. Let the kids help bake or even make their own treats to exchange.

9. Read the Christmas story aloud on Christmas Eve. For families with smaller children, use a nativity set to illustrate the story.

10. Watch a movie series or a succession of each person's favorite video with your family on New Year's Eve. Set an alarm and have bells of all kinds handy so you can ring in the New Year at midnight.

Something to Celebrate

BY MARILYN JANSEN

There, in the presence of the LORD your God, you and your families
shall eat and shall rejoice in everything you have put your hand to,
because the LORD your God has blessed you.

DEUTERONOMY 12:7

otherhood is usually not associated with a life of parties...
with the exception of the occasional princess or pirate birthday bash or family holiday dinner. But it is full of little moments to be celebrated. Why couldn't the appearance of fireflies in spring or successfully putting on a seatbelt without help or transforming a plain ole Wednesday into "Wonderful Wednesday" be the impetus for bubbles and party hats? Everyday blessings are as important to celebrate as birthdays and holidays.

Sometimes in the middle of stress and busyness, however, mothers are hard pressed to find time to breathe, much less throw together a party. But it doesn't require a guest list or catering. All it takes is something to make your children feel special. A song and a dance around the kitchen can change taco night into a fiesta. Notebook paper crowns can make having a cup

of tea with Grandma seem like high tea with the queen. And cupcakes with sprinkles will turn a quiet Christmas Eve snack into a birthday party for Jesus. Simple. Celebratory. Joyous.

Every day the Lord has made is a day to celebrate.

With great joy they celebrated....
GOD had plunged them into a sea of joy.

EZRA 6:22 MSG

Many have forgotten the value and the meaning of traditions.
They are the characteristics and activities which
identify a family as unique and different.

DR. JAMES DOBSON

Tradition is a form of promise from parent to child. It's a way to say,
"I love you," "I'm here for you," and "Some things will not change."

LYNN LUDWICK

In him our hearts rejoice, for we trust in his holy name.

PSALM 33:21

CELEBRATION SCONES

These scones will bring joy to a birthday breakfast, Christmas brunch, or any family celebration.

Ingredients

1 3/4 cups all-purpose flour
1/4 cup sugar
2 teaspoons baking powder
1 teaspoon baking soda
1/4 teaspoon salt
1/4 cup butter, cut in small
    pieces, plus extra for pan
1/2 cup dried cranberries

1/2 cup white chocolate chips
1/2 cup lowfat Greek yogurt
1/3 cup buttermilk

Topping
1 to 2 tablespoons buttermilk
1 teaspoon sugar (raw or
    turbinado is best)

Directions

Preheat oven to 375 degrees. Thinly coat cookie sheet with butter. Stir together flour, sugar, baking powder, baking soda, and salt in large bowl. With pastry blender or fork, cut in butter until mixture resembles coarse crumbs. Stir in cranberries and chips.

Combine yogurt and 1/3 cup buttermilk. Add to dry mixture just until dry ingredients are moistened. Shape dough into ball, place on cookie sheet. With floured fingers press dough or roll dough into 8-inch round. Cut into 8 wedges but do not separate. Brush dough with 1 to 2 tablespoons buttermilk. Sprinkle with sugar.

Bake 15 to 20 minutes or until edges are golden brown. Remove immediately from cookie sheet. Cool 5 minutes before cutting into wedges. Serves 8.

CHAPTER 4

The simple joy of Sharing

If a child is to keep his inborn sense of wonder...he needs the companionship of at least one adult who can share it, rediscovering with him the joy, excitement, and mystery of the world we live in.

RACHEL CARSON

God will generously provide all you need. Then you will always have everything you need and plenty left over to share with others.

2 CORINTHIANS 9:8 NLT

The Blessing of Sharing

BY BONNIE JENSEN

*When you harvest your grain and forget a sheaf back in the field,
don't go back and get it; leave it for the foreigner, the orphan, and the
widow so that GOD, your God, will bless you in all your work.*

DEUTERONOMY 24:19 MSG

How beautiful is an open hand that will give without a moment's
hesitation…and oh, how God's love can be seen in the palm of it.

I remember how my mother taught her six children the way to generosity. She paved it with acts of selflessness and sacrifice. We had very little on the dinner table but could not complain after seeing her give our last few dollars to a needy family, feeling the immediate impact of a powerful truth: "It is more blessed to give than to receive" (Acts 20:35). If we raise our children to be givers, everything they do will be blessed because God keeps His promises.

Giving of our resources is not the only way to be a blessing. Kindness and encouragement are invaluable to a heart in need of a glimpse of God. If we offer a moment to listen, if we speak a kind word, if we go out of our way to help those God brings into our lives or across our path, we create a well of blessing for our children. They will draw from it throughout their lives by way of the memories and joy they've experienced. They will *become* what they've *seen*—vessels of God's grace and goodness—giving and receiving blessings in ways they never imagined.

HOW TO GROW GOOD GIVERS

- Involve your children in discussions about the charities, groups, or missions your family supports.
- As a family, develop weekly, monthly, and yearly giving goals and document them.
- Model—and explain—how the family will budget to meet its giving goals.
- Help your kids divide their money for giving, saving, spending, and investing.
- Encourage kids to develop realistic personal giving goals to support a cause they believe in.

Those who give to the poor will lack nothing.

PROVERBS 28:27

Give Expectantly

BY ROBERTA MESSNER

Without question, the person who has the power
to give a blessing is greater than the one who is blessed.

HEBREWS 7:7 NLT

My great-nephew Trenton was turning eight, and his parents had invited his friends to a party at the local YMCA. As the guests shot hoops on the gleaming oak floor, Trenton's father Alex signaled that it was time for the birthday boy to begin opening his gifts.

Soon I heard a boy with shaggy brown hair whisper to the child standing next to him, "He's opening my gift now!" The box contained a Spiderman wristband, which was greeted by a chorus of "Cool!" "Way to go!" and "Bend your wrist, T. It squirts awesome webs!" The enthusiastic reaction repeated itself as Trenton opened the rest of the presents.

Alex wrapped his arm around my shoulder. "Aren't children terrific when it comes to giving gifts, Aunt Roberta? They're as excited as if they were getting a present themselves."

That evening I drove to the store to pick up a gift for an upcoming bridal shower. *I'll have to paste on a smile*, I thought, *and laugh at the mindless banter while the bride-to-be gushes over mixers and bath towels.*

 But then I remembered the birthday party I'd just attended. What if I chose a gift that I could really get excited about?

I filled a basket with a few of my favorite little household things, like the microfiber cloths that make dusting a breeze and a candle that smells like linen hung on a clothesline in June. When Maria, the bride-to-be, reached for the shrink-wrapped basket tied with a jaunty pink-checked bow, I nudged the woman seated next to me. "That's my gift," I said, and I was really smiling.

When it comes to giving, my prayer is to be ever childlike.

The heart of the giver makes
the gift dear and precious.

MARTIN LUTHER

Each of you must give as you have
made up your mind, not reluctantly
or under compulsion, for God loves
a cheerful giver. And God is able to
provide you with every blessing in
abundance, so that by always having
enough of everything, you may share
abundantly in every good work.

2 CORINTHIANS 9:7–8 NRSV

*The secret of life
is that all we
have and are is
a gift of grace
to be shared.*

LLOYD JOHN OGILVIE

$\mathcal{F}$amilies who practice giving and sharing nurture homes that are filled with joy. Let kindness be a rule. Smile. Appreciate and encourage laughter. Lend a hand to a neighbor in need. Create a habit of selflessness through simple things like encouraging the children to forgo their turn to choose which game the family will play. Suggest they surprise each other with little favors—clean up a mess they didn't make; help with dinner; feed the pets; make all the beds; do a chore they're not asked to do. Anything that changes our focus from *self* to *others* is an act of giving—and in the end it will turn everyone's heart to God.

BONNIE JENSEN

TEN SIMPLE WAYS TO SHARE YOUR BLESSINGS

1. Volunteer at a homeless shelter, soup kitchen, or other charitable organization.
2. Bake cookies or brownies for a neighbor or shut-in.
3. Make your favorite recipe and share the finished product and the recipe with friends.
4. Give your used books away to friends, a church, or a charity.
5. Start a community garden in your neighborhood or contribute to an existing one.
6. Babysit for a single parent.
7. Work with your church to organize a once-a-week potluck dinner for needy families.
8. Clean up a park, schoolyard, or section of sidewalk near you.
9. Read to the blind, the elderly, or those with disabilities.
10. Pray for your neighborhood, town, and school district.

Giving is a joy if we do it in the right spirit.
It all depends on whether we think of it as
"What can I spare?" or as "What can I share?"

ESTHER YORK BURKHOLDER

Everyone was meant to share
God's all-abiding love and care;
He saw that we would need to know
a way to let these feelings show...
So God made hugs.

JILL WOLF

As you know him better, he will give you...
everything you need for living a truly good life:
he even shares his own glory and his own goodness with us!

2 PETER 1:3 TLB

There is no joy in life like the joy of sharing.

BILLY GRAHAM

The Joy of Fireflies

BY SABRA CIANCANELLI

For with you is the fountain of life; in your light we see light.

PSALM 36:9

"Ｔhis is my favorite time of night," my mother said. "Dark enough so you can see the fireflies, light enough so you can catch them. Do you know what lightning bugs are, Solomon?"

My two-year-old looked confused. "I don't think he does," I said.

Outside, the moon showed through the clouds in a dim yellow haze. Crickets chirped. Stray sparks glistened in the field next door. I held Solomon's hand and pointed to the sparks. "Those are lightning bugs!"

"Look at them all!" Mom said.

The sparks of light twinkled above the tall grass. There must have been a hundred of them.

"Well," Mom said, "what are you waiting for? Go catch them!"

Barefoot, I crept over the dew-covered lawn to the field. Arms outstretched, I reached for flashes, grasping at the air. Years disappeared, and I felt the same excitement I'd felt nearly thirty years earlier. The same yard, the same glorious feeling, being with my mom beneath the stars chasing sparks of light. In the darkness, I followed the flashes and then I had one, a tiny little lightning bug safely caught in my hands.

"Look, your mom's got one!" my mother said.

Solomon cheered. "Yeah! Mama's got a light! Mama's got a light!"

Bright yellow twinkled from the creases of my hands.

"That is a firefly, Solomon," my mother said.

"Mommy lights up," he said.

Beneath the stars, we oohed and ahhed as our hands lit up, catching fireflies until it got too dark to see.

Later that night, as I lay in bed, my eyes tired from the cool night air, I felt as if I'd completed a circle: I'd recaptured a favorite childhood memory and made it stronger and brighter by sharing it with my son.

A joy that's shared is a joy made double.

ENGLISH PROVERB

I pray that your hearts will be flooded with light so that you can see something of the future he has called you to share.

EPHESIANS 1:18 TLB

All that I love loses half its pleasure if you are not there to share it.

CLARA ORTEGA

Looking back on all that we've shared and all that is yet to come, I realize that nothing life may offer me could make me happier than a future filled with loving my family.

A Present for My Mother

BY KEITH MILLER

I know, dear God, that you care nothing for the surface—you want us, our true selves—and so I have given from the heart, honestly and happily. And now see all these people doing the same, giving freely, willingly—what a joy!

1 CHRONICLES 29:17 MSG

I was five; my mother's birthday was the next day, so I decided I'd buy her a present. I put the thirty-five cents I'd saved into my pocket, slipped out of the house, and walked the dozen or so blocks to the five-and-ten-cent store. "I want to buy a present for my mother," I told the lady behind the counter.

"How much money do you have?"

I showed her my thirty-five cents.

Nodding seriously, she said, "I see." She showed me some things, but I only shook my head. Then she picked up a little blue glass jar with white bumps all over it and a powder puff inside. Wow! How could that lady have known that Mother had broken a jar just like this one!

"That's it!" Then fear. "What does it cost?"

"Uh...thirty-five cents. Would you like me to wrap it? Wrapping is free."

I carried the little brown sack with the gift-wrapped jar in it all the way home. I was so excited that it didn't seem far at all.

The next day while her friends were having birthday cake and coffee, I gave Mother my present. She was really surprised! Then she asked, "Where did you get this, Keith?"

"I walked to the store to buy it," I said proudly.

"You what?" Suddenly she looked frightened. "Don't ever do that again!"

I cried, and she picked me up. Hugging me, she said, "I love the present, but you shouldn't walk downtown alone." Then she wept and held me until I could wiggle free. As I was running out, I heard one of her friends say, "How in the world did you teach him to do that?" Mother just shook her head. But I knew how. All my life I'd seen my mother giving presents to everyone she knew, and I wanted to be sure she'd get one herself.

If [kids] see, talk, and hear about their parents' charitable giving, they'll be more likely to follow suit.

BRIAN O'CONNELL

Give, and it will be given to you. A good measure, pressed down, shaken together and running over, will be poured into your lap. For with the measure you use, it will be measured to you.

LUKE 6:38

We are called to witness, always with our lives and sometimes with our words, to the great things God has done for us.... This witness must come from a heart that is willing to give without getting anything in return.

HENRI NOUWEN

SHAREABLE SALSA CHICKEN

*Try this simple recipe for delivering to a family in need,
taking to a church function, or sharing with friends at home.*

Ingredients

3 pounds boneless, skinless
    chicken breasts or thighs
1 can cream of chicken soup
1 cup salsa
1 package taco seasoning
1 cup sour cream

1 can black beans, drained
    and rinsed (optional)
Garnishes
    chopped cilantro, shredded
    cheese, diced scallions
    (optional)

Directions

Put chicken, soup, and salsa in slow cooker. Sprinkle taco seasoning over everything. Cook on low for 6 hours. Pull the chicken out and shred with forks; return to slow cooker for another 30 minutes. Stir in beans and sour cream until combined and heat through. Serve over rice or with warm tortillas. Top with garnishes or package them separately if delivering to another family. Serves 8-10.

A word of encouragement to those we meet,
a cheerful smile in the supermarket, a card or letter to a friend,
a readiness to witness when opportunity is given—
all are practical ways in which we may let His light shine through us.

ELIZABETH B. JONES

CHAPTER 5

The simple joy of Love

Is life not full of opportunities for learning love?
Every man and woman every day has a thousand of them.
The world is not a playground, it is a schoolroom.
Life is not a holiday, but an education. And the one
eternal lesson for us all is how better we can love.

HENRY DRUMMOND

*This is my prayer: that your love will flourish and that
you will not only love much but well. Learn to love appropriately.
You need to use your head and test your feelings so that
your love is sincere and intelligent.*

PHILIPPIANS 1:9–10 MSG

Love Is an Anchor

BY BONNIE JENSEN

Love is patient, love is kind. It does not envy, it does not boast, it is not proud. It does not dishonor others, it is not self-seeking, it is not easily angered, it keeps no record of wrongs. Love does not delight in evil but rejoices with the truth. It always protects, always trusts, always hopes, always perseveres. Love never fails.

I CORINTHIANS 13:4–8

To love as God loves is a continual life lesson. While His love is unfailing and unconditional, we are challenged daily by our humanness to give the "always" and "never" kind of love: *always* protects; *always* trusts, *always* hopes, *always* perseveres—*never* fails. Yet, love is the thing most vital to the tender, impressionable spirit of a child. If children feel love and acceptance from us, their view of God's love is strengthened. The world will give them opportunities to doubt—we must give them every reason to believe.

It would be unrealistic to think we will not stumble at times and let our emotions cloud the beauty of God's love for our children, but our mistakes will not change that love. His love, however, should change us. *Always* for the better, *always* for our children, *always* for the hope that they will grow up knowing they are *never* without an anchor for their souls in the storms of life.

Love each other…and take delight
in honoring each other.

ROMANS 12:10 NLT

A mother should love her child the way God loves us.
God says, "I love you regardless of what you do."
It's an unconditional love.

BILL GLASS

GOD told them,
"I've never quit loving you and never will.
Expect love, love, and more love!"

JEREMIAH 31:3 MSG

Let love and faithfulness never leave you;
bind them around your neck,
write them on the tablet of your heart.

PROVERBS 3:3

Glued Together

BY MARY BROWN

Love each other. Just as I have loved you, you should love each other.
JOHN 13:34 NLT

Sometimes I feel overwhelmed by the challenges of parenting. I especially struggle to control my temper. But on my refrigerator is a paper heart, pasted on red construction paper, to remind me of a lesson I learned one February.

That day I just lost it with my then six-year-old daughter—about valentines, of all things! I insisted Elizabeth sign her name to the last three cards for her class. "Elizabeth, there will be no time in the morning to finish before school, so please finish now."

Tears and refusals from Elizabeth. Loud demands from me. She had written her name seventeen times and simply couldn't sign three more. Yes, she could—and must. No, she couldn't—and wouldn't. Angrily, I sent her upstairs to get ready for bed. I tossed the valentines into the box and slammed cupboard doors while cleaning up the kitchen.

Then, clearing papers off the counter, I picked up a worksheet from Sunday school, a page of six hearts with jagged lines through them. Inside each heart was a Bible verse about love. The children could cut out the heart pieces, then match up the Scripture verses to paste them back together.

As I stared at the paper, the verse in the first heart pierced my own: "Love one another, as I have loved you" (John 13:34).

I'd failed to love Elizabeth as God loves me—He's always so patient with my weaknesses, holding back His anger, understanding, and giving constant help! I tiptoed upstairs. "Elizabeth, please forgive me for shouting at you," I said.

To my surprise, she murmured, "Oh, Mom, I'm sorry I didn't want to do what you wanted me to do." With a forgiving hug, our relationship was glued back together.

Our children at times speak a language we may not,
at first, fully understand. And they don't always understand
what we say. But of all the ways we misunderstand one another,
perhaps the most harmful is to not properly communicate love
to our children…. Your child needs to *know* he is loved
in order to grow into a giving, loving, responsible adult.

GARY CHAPMAN AND ROSS CAMPBELL

Above all, love each other deeply,
because love covers over a multitude of sins.

1 PETER 4:8

To be a child is to know the joy of living.
To have a child is to know the beauty of life.

*C*hildren need to feel loved, from the time they're small to the time they're grown, in very much the same ways—from giving hugs to wiping tears to helping hands to listening ears. Love is the place where God meets us and teaches us about each other's hearts and His own. It's a place of refuge, comfort, compassion, and trust, from which we walk away strong and hopeful—knowing He will *always* be our sure foundation.

BONNIE JENSEN

If I speak in the tongues of men or of angels, but do not have love,
I am only a resounding gong or a clanging cymbal.

1 CORINTHIANS 13:1

SIMPLE WAYS TO SAY "I LOVE YOU"

1. Spend time alone weekly with each of your children. Put the date on the family calendar.
2. Let your children overhear you compliment them to someone else.
3. Celebrate everyday accomplishments and simple joys, like tying shoes without help or parallel parking for the first time.
4. When you pack a lunch or snack, add an encouraging note, a heart-shaped cookie, or a piece or two of favorite candy.
5. Read books to your children—even the ones who are old enough to read themselves. Or send a copy of the book you are reading to your grown child so you can read "together."

6. Tell your children stories about their childhood and look at photos or videos from when they were younger.
7. Remind them of something they've taught you and how much you appreciate it.
8. Pray with them and tell God how wonderful it is being their parent.
9. Get to know your children's schedule so you can ask specific questions about their day.
10. Don't allow other things to distract you when your child wants to talk. Really listen. The dishes and that text can wait.
11. Teach your children to do something you loved as a child. Or choose something new to learn together.
12. Bend the rules once in a while. Eating ice cream for breakfast can make a sweet childhood memory.
13. Make the effort to eat dinner together as often as possible. Use the time to let them know how thankful you are for family time.
14. Proudly wear the jewelry and display the artwork your children make for you.
15. Create a secret word, sign, or gesture of affection that only you and your child share—and use it.

*The easiest way of all to tell your kids
that you love them: just say the words.*

KARA FLECK

PRAYER FOR THIS HOUSE

Strengthened by faith, these rafters will
Withstand the battering of the storm;
This hearth, though all the world grow chill,
Will keep us warm....
Laughter shall drown the raucous shout;
And, though these sheltering walls are thin,
May they be strong to keep hate out.
And hold love in.

LOUIS UNTERMEYER

I've loved you the way my Father has loved me.
Make yourselves at home in my love.

JOHN 15:9 MSG

I once asked one of my smaller children what he thought a home
was and he replied, "It's a place where you come in out of the rain."
The home should be a warm sanctuary from the storms of life
for each member of the family. A haven of love and acceptance.

GIGI GRAHAM TCHIVIDJIAN

Sooner or later, we begin to understand that love is more
than verses on valentines and romance in movies.
We begin to know that love is here and now, real and true,
the most important thing in our lives. Love is the creator
of our favorite memories and the foundation of our
fondest dreams. Love is a promise that is always kept,
a fortune that can never be spent, a seed that can flourish
in even the most unlikely of places. And this radiance that
never fades, this mysterious and magical joy that is the
greatest treasure of all—is known only by those who love.

How priceless is your unfailing love, O God!
People take refuge in the shadow of your wings.

PSALM 36:7

Love makes burdens lighter, because you divide them.
It makes joys more intense, because you share them.
It makes you stronger, so that you can reach out and become
involved with life in ways you dared not risk alone.

Love builds memories that endure,
to be treasured up as hints of what shall be hereafter.

BEDE JARRET

Full of Love

BY ROBERTA ROGERS

Since God loved us that much, we surely ought to love each other....
If we love each other, God lives in us,
and his love is brought to full expression in us.

1 JOHN 4:11–12 NLT

*D*oes anyone else have something to share?" Sean Bates, the best man, angled the microphone toward the tables where a hundred and fifty faces, softened by candlelight and glorious fall-color flowers, remained silent after his moving toast to our son John and his bride, Courtney.

"I think I do," I said quietly. He handed me the mic as I rose. Around the dance floor I saw husband and sons—Peter safe from Afghanistan and David just home from Iraq; Tom, newly married himself—and our new daughters, Matti and Susan. There sat brother and nieces and nephews, cousins on both sides, friends I'd known for thirty years and some I'd known just thirty months. There were Courtney's parents, grandparents, aunts, uncles, brother, friends, neighbors. Oh, if only I could stop it all right here—all of us safe and whole and together, laughing, dancing, rejoicing.

"I want to tell you a John story that I think is for all of us here tonight," I began. "One Christmas when he was about seven, Bill and I noticed John wandering from room to room where his brothers were playing and his grandmother and great-aunt were dozing. Then he found his dad and me and tugged us into the kitchen. In his wonderfully earnest way he looked up at us, paused, and said slowly and succinctly, 'This house is full of people I love.'

"Tonight, I think we can all say, 'This house is full of people I love!'"
I leaned over and kissed my newest daughter.

There is nothing quite so deeply satisfying as the solidarity
of a family united across the generations and miles by a common faith and history.

SARA WENGER SHENK

An instant of pure love is more precious to God...than all other good works together, though it may seem as if nothing were done.

ST. JOHN OF THE CROSS

Be filled with love that comes from pure hearts.

1 TIMOTHY 1:5 TLB

Line by line, moment by moment, special times are etched into our memories in the permanent ink of everlasting love in our relationships!

GLORIA GAITHER

He Must Love Me

BY MARY LOU CARNEY

Dear children, let's not merely say that we love each other;
let us show the truth by our actions.

1 JOHN 3:18 NLT

*L*ast night I helped my grandsons get valentines ready for their preschool party. The cards, which featured a variety of bright characters, had to be pulled apart at perforated seams. Small heart stickers were included to hold the folded cards together.

We were pushing the bedtime limit, sitting at the kitchen table in a circle of overhead light. Drake, five, laboriously printed his name over and over on his cards before carefully putting the little stickers on each one. His brother, three, attached heart stickers to his after his daddy wrote BROCK on all of them. My job was licking all sixty-eight envelopes.

Brock finished his stack first, and as he was leaving to go up to bed, he came over to Drake and stuck a red heart sticker on his brother's shirt. Drake stopped his printing and looked at the small bright spot of color on his sleeve. "Look, Nina," he said, "Brock gave me this. He must love me."

Sometimes we grown-ups make love way more complicated than it needs to be. A simple gesture, a kind touch, an unexpected card can all say, "I care about you." And, of course, so can a bright red heart sticker.

In God's wisdom, He frequently chooses to
meet our needs by showing His love toward us
through the hands and hearts of others.

JACK HAYFORD

Anyone who loves God must also love their brother and sister.

1 JOHN 4:21

I am convinced that nothing can ever separate
us from God's love. Neither death nor life,
neither angels nor demons, neither our fears
for today nor our worries about tomorrow—
not even the powers of hell can separate us
from God's love. No power in the sky above
or in the earth below—indeed, nothing in all creation
will ever be able to separate us from the love of God.

ROMANS 8:38–39 NLT

SIMPLE THINGS TO SAY TO YOUR CHILDREN

- I love you.
- You are a gift from God.
- I'm proud of you.
- You can do anything!
- I'm so glad God chose me to be your parent.
- You give me hope for the future.
- God loves you.
- You make my heart smile.
- I will always be here for you.
- I'm praying for you.

A gentle word, like summer rain,
May soothe some heart and banish pain.
What joy or sadness often springs
From just the simple little things!

WILLA HOEY

Love each other deeply with all your heart.

1 PETER 1:22 NLT

CHAPTER 6

The simple joy of the Moment

Not every day of our lives is overflowing with joy and celebration.
But there are moments when our hearts nearly burst within
us for the sheer joy of being alive. The first sight of our
newborn babies, the warmth of love in another's eyes,
the fresh scent of rain on a hot summer's eve—
moments like these renew in us a heartfelt appreciation for life.

GWEN ELLIS

Light-seeds are planted in the souls of God's people,
Joy-seeds are planted in good heart-soil....
Give thanks to our Holy God!

PSALM 97:11–12 MSG

Moments to Treasure

BY BONNIE JENSEN

Lord, help me to realize how brief my time on earth will be.
Help me to know that I am here for but a moment more.

PSALM 39:4 TLB

Our days are collections of moments. Moments bring choices. We make them count by staying in them with full heart and mind. I'm always amazed at how thrilled a child is to have even a few moments of our undivided attention. Faces light up, eyes are engaged, hearts are happy. Moments together can be so beautifully simple, yet incredibly meaningful.

Our time here on earth is for relationship building—foremost, our relationship with God. Beyond that, He orchestrates the symphony of our lives, and our children are among the most important instruments. Created for His glory, each one has a unique place in the harmony of His purpose. Every moment we spend with them—in conversation, prayer, homework, or household chores—gives them confidence in the importance of their *being*.

Time is an expression of love, and it's fleeting and precious. It cannot be bought, only given in moment-by-moment increments. What we spend our minutes on is what matters to us...and there's no greater reward in this world than making our children feel like they matter most.

Time is a very precious gift of God; so precious
that it's only given to us moment by moment.

AMELIA BARR

God works in moments.

FRENCH PROVERB

*Surprise us with love at daybreak;
then we'll skip and dance all the day long.*

PSALM 90:14 MSG

Moments of happiness with your children often
come as a surprise. They seize your heart. Cherish each one;
take the time to make the most of each moment.

Worlds can be found by a child and an adult bending down and looking
together under the grass stems or at the skittering crabs in a tidal pool.

MARY CATHERINE BATESON

Lightning Bugs

BY PAM KIDD

Lift up your eyes and look to the heavens: who created all these?

ISAIAH 40:26

"Want to take an after-dinner walk?" my husband, David, asks.

In my best martyred-fishwife voice I answer, "With half the house left to clean?" To further make my point, I yell down the hall. "Brock! Keri! Don't even think of going to bed until your rooms are cleaned!"

"Oh, Mama," Keri, then six, replies, "we were going to catch lightning bugs."

An hour later, I scan my to-do list and see that, like last week and the week before, the house is reasonably clean. Oops, the porch. Broom in hand, I open the door. The whirr of the vacuum and flying dust have dulled my senses. But one whiff of summer, one glimpse of a single lightning bug, and I'm transported back in time. I recall childhood's cool grass under bare feet and the fresh watermelon smell that hung in the air as I ran through the night reaching for stars. Later, the backyard glider would float like a boat adrift on a secret sea, as I watched luminous lights blinking, blinking, inside a jelly jar.

I walk across the porch, sit on the top step. In the simple dark, I take stock. Do I really want my children to know me as a grouchy mom with a very clean house? Summer was offering an alternative. I hurry inside, take four empty jars from under the sink, and call my glum family of housecleaners together. "I have a problem with lightning bugs," I say. "I need to see if it's still fun to catch them on a summer night." And then, because confession brightens the soul, I add, "I think it might be more important than a clean house."

It was. It still is.

ADVICE FOR CATCHING FIREFLIES

1. Imitate the firefly. Turn off all the lights and shine a flashlight directly up and down or repeat the blinking pattern you see them make.
2. Try using an LED light or covering the flashlight with blue plastic of some sort. Fireflies seem to notice blue light better than other colors.
3. Use a net to catch them so as not to hurt their fragile wings.
4. Put a moistened paper towel in the bottom of a clear jar with a pierced lid for keeping the fireflies. They do better in humid climates.
5. Let them go before going to bed. The best time to release them is evening.

What a wildly wonderful world, GOD! You made it all, with Wisdom at your side, made earth overflow with your wonderful creations.

PSALM 104:24 MSG

God guides us, despite our uncertainties and our vagueness, even through our failings and mistakes.... He leads us step by step, from event to event. Only afterwards, as we look back over the way we have come and reconsider certain important moments in our lives in the light of all that has followed them, or when we survey the whole progress of our lives, do we experience the feeling of having been led without knowing it, the feeling that God has mysteriously guided us.

PAUL TOURNIER

You, LORD, are my lamp; the LORD turns my darkness into light.

2 SAMUEL 22:29

There is not enough darkness in all the world to put out the light of one small candle.... In moments of discouragement, defeat, or even despair, there are always certain things to cling to. Little things usually: remembered laughter, the face of a sleeping child, a tree in the wind— in fact, any reminder of something deeply felt or dearly loved. No one is so poor as not to have many of these small candles. When they are lighted, darkness goes away, and a touch of wonder remains.

ARTHUR GORDON

If you surrender completely to the moments as they pass,
you live more richly those moments.

ANNE MORROW LINDBERGH

Some of the most rewarding and beautiful moments…
happen in the unforeseen open spaces
between planned activities. It is important
that you allow these spaces to exist.

CHRISTINE LEEFELDT

What I'm trying to do here is get you to relax, not be so preoccupied….
People who don't know God and the way he works fuss over these things,
but you know both God and how he works. Steep yourself in God-reality,
God-initiative, God-provisions. You'll find all your everyday human
concerns will be met. Don't be afraid of missing out.

LUKE 12:29–31 MSG

Much of what is sacred is hidden in the ordinary, everyday moments
of our lives. To see something of the sacred in those moments takes
slowing down so we can live our lives more reflectively.

KEN GIRE

The Intensity of the Moment

BY MARILYN MORGAN HELLEBERG

You make known to me the path of life;
you will fill me with joy in your presence,
with eternal pleasures at your right hand.

PSALM 16:11

When our daughter Karen was a baby, I could hardly wait for her to sit up by herself. When she could do that, I started urging her to crawl. When she'd mastered that, I began coaxing her to take her first few faltering steps. Then one day she walked out the door, down the street, and straight into the arms of her kindergarten teacher, while I stood in the doorway wondering where those baby years had gone.

I still jump at the future that way. Instead of savoring my breakfast coffee, I gulp it down so I'll have time for a second cup. Instead of relishing the warmth and stimulation of my shower, I'm planning what to wear that day. While I'm eating my meatloaf, I've got my eye on the lemon pie. All day, I seem to live just a step ahead of the present moment. But at a recent prayer retreat, we practiced trying to be really present in the now.

We started with our morning prayers. We centered our thoughts on God for the whole prayer period. Two minutes of steady presence, we found, were better than fifteen minutes of meandering mind. Since that time, I've become aware that each moment has its own intensity—and reward—if I'll only give myself over to it.

A simple life is the result of living joyfully in the moment—
of being present in this moment and not wishing for the next
or regretting the last. Simply enjoy each moment as it comes.

Guard well your spare moments. They are like uncut diamonds.
Discard them, and their value will never be known. Improve them,
and they will become the brightest gems in a useful life.

RALPH WALDO EMERSON

We throw open our doors to God and discover at the same
moment that he has already thrown open his door to us.
We find ourselves standing where we always hoped we might stand—
out in the wide open spaces of God's grace and glory,
standing tall and shouting our praise.

ROMANS 5:2 MSG

*Father, may I honor this moment, using it for what
I value most, like the rarest of rainbows, so soon gone.*

MARILYN MORGAN HELLEBERG

In the Blink of a Moment

We think we have to plan special time with our children, when actually, chances to pause and make wonderful moments present themselves throughout the day. Every second spent inside a hug is priceless—give them often and freely. "*I love you*" takes seconds. The minutes that begin and end each day have significant impact—push everything else aside to fill them with tenderness and love. We blink, and moments are gone—if we forget their worth, our children might forget how valuable *they* are.

BONNIE JENSEN

You will find as you look back upon your life,
that the moments when you have really lived are the
moments when you have done things in the spirit of love.

HENRY DRUMMOND

Gratitude bestows reverence, allowing us to encounter everyday
epiphanies, those transcendent moments of awe that
change forever how we experience life and the world.

JOHN MILTON

MAKE MOMENTS TO CHERISH

1. Celebrate the "firsts" in life with certificates, medals, or photos.
2. Use the good china for the usual weeknight meal once in a while and talk about the best moments of the day, week, or month.
3. Send a thank-you note through the mail to your child for something they have done for you.
4. Glue photos of your kids in your gratitude journal and tell them how thankful you are for them.
5. Worry less about a messy house and play games with your children.
6. Identify one simple joy in each day and point it out to your kids.
7. Take a photo of your child doing something "normal" like feeding the cat, drying the dishes, or hugging a family member to frame that moment in time.
8. Take time out of a busy day for high tea at the kids' table, letting them set the menu and pour the tea/water/milk/lemonade.
9. As your child brings worries or joys to your attention, seize the opportunity to incorporate prayer into the conversation.
10. While running errands, make a detour and have a five-minute teeter-totter or swing contest in the local playground.

Road to Happiness

BY KELLY BASS

Our steps are made firm by the LORD,
when he delights in our way;
though we stumble, we shall not fall headlong,
for the LORD holds us by the hand.

PSALM 37:23–24 NRSV

My husband, Joe, and I had been driving for an hour, our Honda packed to the max with our son, audiobooks, video games, suitcases, and snacks, when my back began to ache. I shifted uncomfortably. Thirteen hours to go.

"This is going to be our best vacation ever," Joe said. *Really?* I thought.

When Joe had first proposed this trip to the Grand Canyon, I was excited. In all our married life, we'd never taken a family vacation far from our home.

His reason for taking this trip was eight-year-old Chandler. When Joe was that age, his parents took him to the Grand Canyon, driving from Oklahoma, stopping at every historical marker along the way.

"It was the best time I ever had," he said one night after we'd put our son to bed, "and I want it to be Chandler's best time too." I was with him 100 percent. Until Joe said we'd be driving.

To me, there are two parts to vacation: the hassle of getting there and the joys of your destination. I'd taken long-distance car trips as a child, and the memories they stirred were nothing like Joe's. What I remembered were the predawn starts that left me feeling like a zombie, eating warm bologna sandwiches for lunch, and being squished in the backseat between my siblings and the luggage.

Our first hour on the road hadn't been so bad. Chandler was in the backseat, headphones on, listening to an audiobook. Hank Williams Jr. crooned on the radio while Joe and I chatted. But after a while I started to fidget.

"Wanna stop and stretch?" Joe asked.

"No, thanks," I said. The fewer stops, the faster we'd get there.

We pushed on across Oklahoma. Around sunset we neared the Texas border, a palette of reds, pinks, indigos, and oranges tinting the fields and lighting the horizon. We passed a farmhouse with a windmill; it rose like a church steeple, its blades turning in the prairie breeze.

"Look how pretty that is," Joe said.

But my mind was elsewhere. I'm the organizer in the family. It was almost dinnertime. "We have to find somewhere to eat," I said. "Any ideas?"

"Relax, we'll find a place," Joe said.

That was how the entire day had gone, Joe admiring the view, Chandler listening to an audiobook, occasionally joining in his dad's oohs and aahs. "I never knew the country was so big!" he exclaimed.

Me? I kept fidgeting. I was checking my watch or map so I could plan our next stop or recalculate the number of hours to our destination.

We found a place for dinner near the motel where we (finally!) stopped for the night. I have to say the food tasted great.

The next morning I suggested we play the alphabet game, where you point out letters on roadside billboards. Chandler was first to spot the letter Z. "Arizona!" he shouted, pointing to a sign. I gave him a high five. I couldn't remember the last time the three of us had laughed so hard together. I checked my watch. *Wow, time has flown. In a few hours, we'll be there.*

Mid-afternoon we reached Williams, Arizona, where we'd hop a train to the Canyon. The main street was straight out of a Hollywood Western, complete with hitching posts, a general store, and wood-plank sidewalks. "Let's go explore the town," Joe said, excited. The guys started across the street. I checked my watch. Forty-five minutes before the train was due. I didn't want to miss it. "I'll wait at the depot," I said.

Just then two wranglers walked onto the dusty street. Words were exchanged. A crowd gathered—costumed townsfolk. This was rehearsed! Joe hoisted Chandler on his shoulders so he could see.

The wrangler sporting leather chaps and a handlebar mustache fingered his gun. The other wriggled his fingers. Both drew and fired. The one in the chaps fell, sprawling in the dust. Right then, the train to the Grand Canyon pulled in. Joe and Chandler jogged across the street, and we boarded. On our way at last!

But my guys weren't thinking about the Grand Canyon at all. "Mom," Chandler said, "that shootout was so cool!"

That's when it hit me. Joe was right. Our vacation wasn't just starting. We'd been on holiday all along. *Lord, it's the journey, not the destination, right? Is that the message?*

We were near the Canyon, but it no longer seemed so important. I smiled at Joe and Chandler. They couldn't stop talking about the shootout. I joined in. The way I felt, it was the highlight of our vacation...so far.

CHAPTER 7

The simple joy of Family

If we truly want peace in the world, let us begin by loving one another in our own families. If we want to spread joy, we need for every family to have joy.

MOTHER TERESA

I have no greater joy than to hear that my children are walking in the truth.

3 JOHN 1:4

The Love of Family

BY BONNIE JENSEN

*The LORD is good. His unfailing love continues forever,
and his faithfulness continues to each generation.*

PSALM 100:5 NLT

*E*very family dynamic is different, and every member holds a special place no one else can fill. God uses families to teach our hearts to love and accept without condition, to forgive without hesitation, to see others as valuable and unique. I am nothing like my sisters, but I couldn't imagine going through life void of the lessons we taught each other.

Home is where laughter comes easily, comfort is most welcome, where tears flow freely, and love runs deeply. Families are created by God for His purposes, and none are by chance. When we're there for each other, when we choose our words wisely, when we say "I'm sorry" and "I forgive you," when "I love you" is said often—each brick of the family foundation is strengthened. This is what God intended every child to have—the same firm footing His love gives to us.

So when things get hectic, when mistakes are made, challenges come, and days are trying, remember: *The Lord is good. His unfailing love continues*…and so must ours. Be good to each other, always, for God puts families together in His way for His reasons—the most important one being for His glory.

Other things may change us,
but we start and end with family.

ANTHONY BRANDT

Peace and prosperity to you, your family, and everything you own!

1 SAMUEL 25:6 NLT

Moments shared with family blend together in sweet harmonies—
a melody of peace and happiness to carry in our hearts always.

I know now that I was a child placed in the protection of
my mother and father, and all that I learned about peace and nature
and the size of the moon, I learned in the backyard.

CHRISTOPHER DE VINCK

Family Noise

BY KAREN VALENTIN

How good and pleasant it is when God's people live together in unity!
PSALM 133:1

After packing a bag with toys, diapers, baby clothes, bottles, and who knows how many other things, my son and I head out the door for a weekend in the country. Like most city moms, I have no trouble lifting the hefty stroller up and down the subway stairs, and at Penn Station I purchase a ticket for the train that will whisk us away from Manhattan. After one transfer and more stairs, we settle into our seats for the two-hour trip.

As I look out the window, skyscrapers give way to mountains and trees, and I know that the long, troublesome journey will be worth it. Much more than the country air, it's the family waiting for my arrival that I'm looking forward to. My cousin will honk his horn with a wave, my sister will jump out of the car and tackle me with hugs, and my niece and nephews will run straight to the stroller, shouting my son's name.

When I was growing up in Brooklyn, every day was crowded with the sweet chaos of family, and I'd always envisioned my own children as part of it. But slowly, everyone moved away—my parents to Florida and everyone else hours north of New York City. I miss the family circus and long for my son to experience the abundance of love I enjoyed as a child. So when the voices of my husband and me are not enough and the apartment seems too quiet, I pack a bag and take the train to the love and noise of my family.

Our family is a blessing
It means so many things
Words could never really tell
the joy our family brings....
Our family is heartfelt pride
the feeling deep and strong
that makes us glad to take a part
and know that we belong.

MARGARET FISHBACK POWERS

Let your unfailing love surround us,
LORD, for our hope is in you alone.

PSALM 33:22 NLT

We must be proactive in building family closeness.
Children see parental presence as a reflection of our love and care.
Simple traditions such as eating dinner together, game night, going for ice cream, no-TV nights, or anything that encourages uninterrupted time together, will foster a well-connected, healthy family. Children learn they are valued when we spend time with them. It will increase joy and instill confidence in them as they grow, while making memories they'll keep for a lifetime.

BONNIE JENSEN

TEN TIPS FOR SECURING FAMILY TIME

1. Keep a family calendar in a central location. Each month put "family time" appointments on it in permanent ink. Some possibilities are: a movie night, a video game/activity tournament, a day at a museum, a scavenger hunt at home or at a park.
2. Always have a treat or fun activity included in scheduled events so family members will want to participate. Take into consideration each family member's likes and dislikes.
3. Plan family get-aways like vacations, camping trips, and reunions in advance and ask everyone for input. Then circle the dates in bright colors on the calendar.
4. Help each other with chores. It's more fun, and they get done faster.
5. Play games together once a week. A quick game of HORSE, a board

game, dominoes, or even a video game can strengthen family bonds.

6. Eat out or eat "simply" once a week so that your family can spend time talking to each other instead of spending time on meal preparation and cleanup.

7. Seize family opportunities whenever they arrive—even if they aren't on the calendar. A canceled practice can make way for an unexpected family bike ride or a trip to an ice cream shop.

8. Build excitement for family outings by counting down to them. A daily reminder of upcoming events or notes with the details placed on their plate at dinner time will remind the whole family of the fun time coming soon.

9. As a family, draw or build a family tree. As you fill in names, discuss each person, what you admire about them, what characteristics you share with them, where they live, etc.

10. Invite God into your activities by praying for them in advance and asking His blessing as you begin your time together.

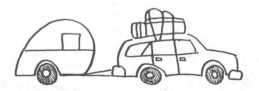

Play Clothes

BY MELODY BONNETTE

So I commend the enjoyment of life,
because nothing is better for a person under the sun.

ECCLESIASTES 8:15

I rushed home from work to babysit Indy and Noah, my two grand-sons. I hadn't seen them much lately. I was juggling my job, school, housework, and gardening. There was no time for anything else.

I was still in my business suit and heels when they arrived. Four-year-old Indy grabbed my hand, ready to run to the pond to feed the ducks.

"Grandma," he said excitedly, "go get your play clothes on!"

"Oh, Indy," I laughed, "I don't have any play clothes."

He looked at me wide-eyed. "What do you wear when you play?"

It was the third time that week the issue of play had come up. When a deliveryman hustled to my door with a package, I joked that he was as busy as I was. He smiled and said that the key to life is to remember to find time to play, too. I responded with a blank stare.

It came up again two days later at a seminar. When asked to create a personal schedule that included time for me to do something just for fun, I came up empty-handed.

The following Saturday afternoon when the boys came over, I wore my newly labeled play clothes—jogging pants, tie-dyed T-shirt, and tennis shoes. I took their little hands in mine, and we ran to the back-yard—not to weed the garden, not to rake the leaves, and not to do homework at the patio table, but simply to play.

Fortunate are the people whose roots are deep.

AGNES MEYER

They will be like a tree planted by the water that sends out its roots by the stream. It does not fear when heat comes; its leaves are always green. It has no worries in a year of drought and never fails to bear fruit.

JEREMIAH 17:8

There are two lasting bequests we can give our children. One of these is roots; the other, wings.

HODDING CARTER III

What families have in common the world around is that they are the place where people learn who they are and how to be that way.

JEAN ILLSLEY CLARKE

Unexpected Dividends

BY SUSAN M. BLAKE

Open my eyes so I can see what you show me of your miracle-wonders.

PSALM 119:18 MSG

My teenage son asked me to come out into the frigid winter night to see Jupiter through his telescope. Bill had become very interested in astronomy. Here in Alaska, stars are not visible in summer but are brilliant in the deep nights of winter. The only chance he had of seeing anything was when it was clear and very cold.

I was not anxious to get all my down gear on to go out and look at a blob in the sky. The spotting scope wasn't strong enough to see much. But he was so excited, I couldn't turn him down.

Outside, the night air was so cold I could hardly breathe. Bill lined up the telescope for me. I looked through and there was the blob of light I could see with the naked eye, only bigger.

"Adjust it, Mom," he said impatiently. I turned the dial, and suddenly it came into complete focus. Floating around Jupiter were three tiny bright moons! I was amazed and excited. I'd never seen a planet like that before.

Isn't it astounding how often, when you put your own inclinations aside and do something to please somebody else, unexpected dividends flow into your life?

Bless—that's your job, to bless.
You'll be a blessing and also get a blessing.

1 PETER 3:9 MSG

Bringing up a family should be an adventure,
not an anxious discipline in which everybody is graded for performance.

MILTON R. SAPIRSTEIN

The Lord will reward each one of us for the good we do.

EPHESIANS 6:8 NLT

*When you look at your life,
the greatest happinesses are family happinesses.*

DR. JOYCE BROTHERS

The joy that you give to others is the joy that comes back to you.

JOHN GREENLEAF WHITTIER

KEY QUALITIES OF THRIVING FAMILIES

Research has revealed that strong relationships at home and in the community are more important to thriving families than just about any other factor. The key qualities that contribute to strong families are:

- Positive communication: listen carefully, speak respectfully
- Affection: show warmth
- Emotional openness: share feelings
- Support for individual interests/talents: encourage each other
- Family meals: eat together most days
- Shared activities: be active together
- Meaningful traditions: celebrate holidays and family milestones
- Dependability: expect each other to be there daily
- Openness about tough topics: discuss sensitive issues openly
- Fair rules: set reasonable rules and consequences
- Defined boundaries: set limits on time and activities
- Clear expectations: openly express expectations
- Contributions to family responsibilities: do your chores
- Management of daily commitments: balance home, school, work
- Adaptability: be flexible
- Problem solving: work together
- Democratic decision making: ask for everyone's opinions
- Neighborhood cohesion: look out for one another
- Relationships with others: connect with teachers, coaches, leaders
- Enriching activities: participate in programs and activities
- Supportive resources: make help available

ADAPTED FROM THE SEARCH INSTITUTE

CHAPTER 8

The simple joy of Gratitude

To be grateful is to recognize the love of God
in everything He has given us—and He has given us
everything. Every breath we draw is a gift of His love,
every moment of existence is a gift of grace.

THOMAS MERTON

Praise the LORD! Give thanks to the LORD, for he is good!
His faithful love endures forever. Who can list the glorious miracles
of the LORD? Who can ever praise him enough?

PSALM 106:1–2 NLT

Gratitude Is the Key

BY BONNIE JENSEN

Let the peace of God rule in your hearts…and be thankful.
COLOSSIANS 3:15 NKJV

The key to being ever grateful is getting into the habit of appreciating little things. Being greeted with a smile and a hug, recognizing someone's excitement to see you, having a child who is always thankful to love you and to be loved back. Walking in the park, holding hands, the wriggling of tiny toes in the sand, snuggling at bedtime, trading good-night kisses—all moments of love, sweet in God's sight.

These are the precious moments that make up our days, the ones we need to keep our eyes and hearts wide open to see. God is in them. We honor Him by savoring each one. We bless Him by being thankful for and with our children—they are gifts from His hand. Routines, busyness, and daily responsibilities squeeze in and bear down, competing for our time and energy. We need only to stop and pay attention to what we've been given, to what is right in front of us, to be truly thankful.

Gratitude, like joy, is contagious. One leads to the other. Children who learn to be thankful grow up to be happy. They look for the goodness of God in the details of life—a whispered prayer answered, a sunny day, a cozy bed, a loving home. Even in the midst of trials, if we focus on being thankful at all times, our children will learn to trust that God works everything together for good.

Pray diligently. Stay alert,
with your eyes wide open in gratitude.

COLOSSIANS 4:2 MSG

A child of God should be a visible beatitude for joy and happiness,
and a living doxology for gratitude and adoration.

CHARLES H. SPURGEON

The joy of receiving is in far more than the gifts.
When we receive graciously and gladly, we reciprocate the gift
with joy and gratitude; in that moment of shared happiness
and understanding, giver and receiver connect.

Prompted by Gratitude

BY MARION BOND WEST

[Give] thanks to God the Father for everything.

EPHESIANS 5:20

One cold night I stopped by my twin sons' room to check on them before going to bed. They both appeared to be asleep. However, Jon murmured, "Cold, Mama." Checking in their closet, I couldn't find a blanket, so I slipped off my bathrobe and covered Jon with it. In the moonlight that came in through the window, I carefully tucked it under his feet and chin. He was so still and quiet, I was sure he was asleep.

The boys were nearly eleven, and I didn't often tuck them in at night. I went on down the dark hall to my bed and climbed in wearily. It had been a long, hard day. I knew I'd be asleep within minutes.

"Mama," came the call from the boys' room. I sighed, hoping Jon didn't need anything else.

"Yes?"

In a tone, soft for Jon, he said, "It was nice when you took off your robe and gave it to me and even tucked me in. Thanks."

The unexpected thanks from my son touched my heart and caused me to smile in the darkness. My boys seldom expressed gratitude. I was always after them to say thank you.

"You're welcome," I answered. "'Night. Sweet dreams," I added happily.

And then I didn't go right to sleep. Instead, I thought about how Jon's thanking me for such a little thing had pleased me. Prompted by his gratitude, I began to thank my Father for many little things I'd neglected to say thanks for through the day.

Help me, O LORD…that I might sing
praises to you and not be silent.
O LORD my God, I will give you
thanks forever!

PSALM 30:10–12 NLT

*Every day shared
with the ones we love
is a gift for which we
are very thankful!*

Our family is a unit that is not
shared by everyone. It is ours by design,
by tradition, by growth. We love and
protect it in our own special way.

JANETTE OKE

Heavenly Father,
Thank You for my wonderful family. Even though we are not perfect,
I praise You for this group of people that You have ordained as those
who will be closest to me. Help me to be the best wife, mother,
and woman that I can be—today and every day of my life. Amen.

KIM BOYCE.

FIFTEEN WAYS TO SAY THANKS

There are many ways to show gratitude, from just saying the words to buying gifts. The best way to teach children to be grateful is by letting them see you give thanks. When we involve them, we are setting them up to live lives of gratitude.

Here are some ideas to help you show gratitude to those who have helped you and to model thanksgiving to your children.

1. Send a heartfelt thank-you note or card. Let your children sign it, lick the envelope, or put on the stamp.

2. During family prayers, thank God for those who have blessed you. Encourage your children to give thanks in their own words.

3. Go out of your way to give a hug and say, "Thank you!" Do this with your kids when they have helped you.

4. Give something homemade or home-baked from a mix or the refrigerator section of the market. Let your children help open packages, stir, set the timer, or decorate.

5. Give fresh flowers either from your garden or your floral department/shop. Include a card with a heartfelt message. A child can pick flowers, tie on a bow, or make the card.

6. Take the person out for coffee, tea, or lunch. Include your kids if appropriate or take them out when they deserve a thank-you.

7. Offer your services: If they need food, offer to cook a meal. If you can paint, help them remodel. Mow. Shop. Wash the car. Watch the dog. Let your children participate if age appropriate.

8. Give a list of all the things you are grateful for—their friendship, their prayers, their dedication, their help. Let your child make his/her own list to give.

9. Give a gift, something homemade or something inexpensive that you know they will like. Ask your child's opinion on what is a good gift.

10. Bring them a plant for their yard or windowsill. Adding a label written by your child will make it more special.

11. Reciprocate. Do for them what they did for you. Ask your children what nice things others have done for them and make plans to reciprocate.

12. Attend the events that are important to them. If they sing, go to their concert. Take your children with you so they can appreciate the talent/skill/dedication.

13. Leave little notes in unexpected places. A quick thank-you written with soap on a mirror can change someone's day. Let your kids write the same kinds of notes for family members.

14. Spend time with them. Sometimes it is as simple as taking a few minutes to be fully with someone. Help your children understand "being all there."

15. Pray for them. Find out what prayer needs they have and let them know you will pray for them. Include your children in the prayer. They often have a unique perspective to add.

Josh's Light

BY SHERYL ANDERSON

We'll never comprehend all the great things he does;
his miracle-surprises can't be counted.

JOB 9:10 MSG

*J*osh had talked about this night for weeks, the night of the middle-school Christmas pageant. From our seats in the auditorium, my husband and I scanned the sea of red- and green-clad students on the stage, looking for our oldest son. "There he is," my husband whispered. Josh stood directly in the center of the chorus risers, smiling. He seemed right at home among the other seventh and eighth graders. At first glance, you wouldn't know Josh has Down syndrome. He'd practiced all semester with his special education teachers and the choir director so he could sing in the concert with the rest of the students. How would he react now that he was actually in the spotlight? He was especially excited about the last song, when each student would light a candle, one after the other. "Just wait, Mom. You'll love it," he promised.

All I wanted was for the night to go well. Throughout his school career, Josh had always had a teacher's aide by his side. In art class, gym, lunch—someone was watching out for him. Tonight he was on his own. His special ed teacher, sitting in front of us, turned around. "He'll do fine, Mrs. Anderson," she said, squeezing my hand. I smiled and thanked her.

I hope she's right, I thought. The house lights dimmed. The choir started up, and Josh's face beamed as his voice joined the others. No one would notice one child singing a little off-key or coming in slightly late. I relaxed a bit in my seat as the kids sang their carols.

The time came for the big finale. Candles were passed among the choir members. The song began. A student at each end of the risers lit a candle and touched the flame to the candle of the next student. Every second or so, another student's face was illuminated by candlelight. Slowly, the lit candles worked their way toward Josh. Our neighbor's grandson, Victor, stood to his right. He lit his own candle and turned to light Josh's.

Josh's wick wouldn't catch. As hard as Victor tried, Josh's candle stayed dark. Frustrated, Victor shook his head—he was giving up. Josh's smile faded and my heart sank. Every student sang, every face beamed through the warm glow of the candles. Except for my Josh. *In this, too, Lord?* I cried silently. *Even now he has to be singled out from all the others?* I stared at the floor and tried to hide my tears.

My husband gave me a nudge. "Look," he whispered. On Josh's left was an older boy we didn't know. He was trying to light the stubborn candle. No luck. The boy paused then did something I didn't expect.

He took Josh's unlit candle and exchanged it for his own lit one. Josh promptly raised the candle up, illuminating the restored smile on his face. A wave of gratitude swept over me. The other boy managed to pinch the wax away from the wick and got it to light, and finally, the whole chorus was shining bright.

We witnessed a Christmas miracle that night. That boy wanted Josh to have his own light, even if it meant giving up his own. In that one simple act, God showed us that everyone has an opportunity to shine.

I will thank the LORD with all my heart.

PSALM 111:1 NLT

You're here to be light, bringing out the God-colors in the world…. Shine! Keep open house; be generous with your lives. By opening up to others, you'll prompt people to open up with God, this generous Father in heaven.

MATTHEW 5:14, 16 MSG

Thankfulness is the soil in which joy thrives.

Gratitude is the inward feeling of kindness received.
Thankfulness is the natural impulse to express that feeling.
Thanksgiving is the following of that impulse.

HENRY VAN DYKE

FOR MOTHER

For childhood's golden memories
For happy bygone years
The comfort of your presence
In days of joy or tears
For all your love upon life's way—
I thank you from my heart this day.

When we start to count flowers,
we cease to count weeds;
When we start to count blessings,
we cease to count needs;
When we start to count laughter,
we cease to count tears;
When we start to count memories,
we cease to count years.

Everything God created is good, and to be received with thanks....
God's Word and our prayers make every item in creation holy.

1 TIMOTHY 4:4–5 MSG

Thank You, God, for knowing us so well. When our little problems seem
too tiny to bring to You, remind us that You care about every aspect of
our lives. When the little things grow and become really big problems,
remind us that we can cast all our cares on You. Thank You for being
dependable, for caring about every aspect of our lives, for helping us
through every situation. You fill our hearts with gratitude. Amen.

MARILYN JANSEN

Are not two sparrows sold for a penny? Yet not one of them
will fall to the ground outside your Father's care.

MATTHEW 10:29

A Little Gratitude

BY SANDRA WIGGINS STANGE

I will give thanks to you, LORD, with all my heart;
I will tell of all your wonderful deeds.

PSALM 9:1

One afternoon, as I bent to remove clothes from the dryer, a searing pain ripped through my back. I froze, pretzel-like. Frantically, I massaged my knotted muscles until I was able to straighten up, but the pain was still intense.

By evening, I was worried. In a few days, guests were coming to stay at our house. With dozens of chores to do, I didn't have time to go to the doctor or lie around! Wincing, I stepped into the shower, turned on the hot water full force, and began to pray. "Oh, Lord, You've just got to take away this pain. Please, please, make me better."

The next morning, though some minor pain still lingered, getting around was much easier. Gradually I slipped into my usual routine, and by lunchtime my back trouble was completely forgotten.

About mid-afternoon my teenage son, Dave, burst in noisily from school. "Mom, you've just gotta get the grass stains out of my softball uniform before the game tonight!"

Sighing stoically, I took his shirt and pants.

A couple of hours later, as my husband, Ron, came in from work, Dave dashed out the door past him, his clean, dry uniform slung over his arm. "Hi, Dad," he called hurriedly. "Bye, Mom." And he was gone.

"Can you believe that kid?" I fumed. "He didn't even bother to thank me for rubbing my fingers almost raw on those pants! He sure doesn't mind asking favors, but show a little gratitude? Oh, no, he doesn't have time for that!"

"Well, honey," Ron said, "what's new? Most kids are ungrateful. They take it for granted that their parents will come running every time they call." Then he eyed me appraisingly. "Well, you seem to be moving around again with your old zip. Your back must be better."

My back?

The twinge I felt was not in my back. It was in my conscience. Who was I to complain about children taking favors for granted?

"Yes, my back is fine now," I murmured to Ron as I turned off the burner under the pork chops. "I'll be back in a minute. I have to take care of something before I put dinner on."

It seemed fitting to return to the place where God had so patiently listened to me earlier. In the privacy of the bathroom, I bowed my head. *Lord, thank You for taking away my pain. And forgive me for being such an ungrateful child.*

CHOCOLATE TORTE

This is a decadent but easy and perfect-for-giving dessert that says, "I am really, really grateful!" It also makes a great Thanksgiving or holiday treat.

Ingredients
- 1/2 package sugar cookie dough (18 ounce size)
- 1/4 cup cocoa powder
- 10 tablespoons unsalted butter, plus extra to butter pan
- 8 ounces bittersweet chocolate chips
- 2 large eggs plus one large egg yolk
- 1/4 cup sugar
- Whipped cream

Directions

Preheat convection oven to 325° (350° for conventional oven). Place rack in bottom position if using a convection oven, middle position for conventional oven.

Butter torte pan.

Combine cookie dough and cocoa. Press into a flat disk. Place between two pieces of plastic wrap and roll into a 12-inch circle (big enough for bottom and sides of torte pan). Remove top piece of wrap and carefully flip exposed dough onto torte pan. Ease into pan. Remove top plastic. Press extra dough into cracks or holes.

Combine butter and chocolate in microwave-safe bowl. Heat for 1 minute. Stir well. Heat for 15-second intervals until big chunks are almost melted. Stir to finish melting. Cool completely.

Whisk eggs, yolk, and sugar together. Gradually whisk cooled chocolate mixture into eggs.

Place crust in oven and bake until set—about 4 minutes for convection oven, about 9 for conventional oven. Pour filling into crust, smooth with spatula, and return to oven for 6 more minutes (8 minutes for conventional oven), until barely set.

Cool completely. Dust top of torte with cocoa. Serve with whipped cream. Serves 16.

CHAPTER 9

The simple joy of Laughter

Heavenly Father,
Thank You for this season of my life when I have children around
to make me laugh. May I always find joy in the words and actions
of my children. Allow me to experience the happiness of being
young and carefree with my little ones. Amen.

KIM BOYCE

God has made me laugh, and all that hear will laugh with me.

GENESIS 21:6 NKJV

Laughter Is the Best Medicine

BY BONNIE JENSEN

The joy of the LORD is your strength.

NEHEMIAH 8:10

*T*here is nothing else like the sheer delight of laughing with children. The sound of a giggling child is the remedy for any burden the day may bring. It is medicine for the soul and has even been described as "internal aerobics." Videos of parents making their babies laugh out loud garner millions of views on the Internet because laughter induces laughter—and everyone loves how it makes them feel.

Laughter is an expression of joy. When we choose to immerse ourselves in God's joy, it makes its way into our attitude, our countenance, and our children. In spite of spilled milk, last-minute projects, missing the bus, sibling spats, or any of the many things that can disrupt our "joy flow," we can choose to smile, laugh, and lighten the mood. It's amazing how quickly the tide turns from tension to contentment when we get into the habit of being cheerful.

Laugh with your children. Make them laugh. Be silly. Forget you're grown up. Love and appreciate their joy-lit faces. Life is going to bring big battles their way, and you want them to know that God is bigger than any trouble, and joy is their strength.

The sound of children laughing as they run ahead of me is,
I think, one of life's great pleasures.

CHRISTOPHER DE VINCK

Surely you all know that my joy comes from your being joyful.

2 CORINTHIANS 2:3 NLT

A mother's love endures through all...she remembers...
[her child's] merry laugh, the joyful shout of his childhood,
the opening promise of his youth.

WASHINGTON IRVING

*We are all here for a spell, get all
the good laughs you can.*

WILL ROGERS

Falling into Laughter

BY MARION BOND WEST

There is a time for everything…a time to laugh.
ECCLESIASTES 3:1, 4

I was babysitting three of my grandchildren, and it was time to bathe two-year-old Thomas. I got him and all his toys into the tub and began to wash him, sitting at an angle on the edge so I could continue talking with Jamie and Katie, his sisters. Then, before I could catch myself, I lost my balance, slipped backward, and fell into the tub—fully clothed.

My granddaughters laughed hysterically. Thomas, observing them for a few seconds, threw his head back and joined in the laughter. As I sat in the warm water with my arms and legs extended, I felt this tremendous laugh making its way out. I leaned against the pink tiles and let it come. The four of us were joined together by our laughter, which lasted for perhaps three minutes and was exhausting and satisfying and unforgettable.

Of course, I wouldn't have laughed in my young motherhood days. I would have resented anything that made me look less than perfect. I would have been in a nasty mood for the rest of the evening, probably not speaking. And we would never have mentioned the incident again.

I'm glad I have finally learned—through experience, age, and God's grace—that there's a time to laugh, even at myself and my humanness.

Laughing at ourselves as well as with each other gives
a surprising sense of togetherness.

HAZEL C. LEE

Humor is one of God's most marvelous gifts.
Humor gives us smiles, laughter, and gaiety. Humor reveals
the roses and hides the thorns. Humor makes our heavy burdens
light and smoothes the rough spots in our pathways.

SAM ERVIN

*God is at home in the play of His
children. He loves to hear us laugh.*

PETER MARSHALL

I have God's more-than-enough, more joy in one ordinary day....
At day's end I'm ready for sound sleep, for you, GOD,
have put my life back together.

PSALM 4:7–8 MSG

*L*aughter is the best aerobic exercise, working muscles all over the body and increasing blood flow to the heart. According to William Fry, a professor at Stanford University, California, one minute of laughter equals ten minutes on the rowing machine.

A cheerful heart is good medicine.

PROVERBS 17:22

A happy heart is the best service we can give to God.

MARIE CHAPIAN

Grace creates liberated laughter. The grace of God...is beautiful, and it radiates joy and awakens humor.

KARL BARTH

Prayer and laughter. I learned both by example from my parents.

JOE GARAGIOLO

LAUGH WITH A CHILD

Sometimes the simple joy of laughter is all we need to change the course of our day. Bring some laughter to your day by sharing some of these jokes with your children or grandchildren.

Where does spaghetti go to dance?
To the Meat Ball.

A third-grade teacher was getting to know her students on the first day of school. She turned to one little girl and asked, "What does your daddy do?" The girl replied, "Whatever my mommy tells him to do."

Where do snowmen keep their money?
In snowbanks.

What kind of shoes do you make with banana peels?
Slippers!

A little boy covered in dirt came in from playing in the yard and asked his mother, "Who am I?" Ready to play the game she said, "I don't know. Who are you?" "Wow!" cried the child. "Mrs. Johnson was right. She said I was so dirty, my own mother wouldn't recognize me!"

What's a shark's favorite game?
Swallow the leader.

Healing Laughter

BY REBECCA ONDOV

Therefore, as we have opportunity, let us do good to all.

GALATIANS 6:10 NKJV

I stacked the breakfast dishes on my arm. As I turned to take them into the kitchen, I almost ran into Sarah, an adorable eight-year-old guest, who stood squeezing her cowboy hat with both hands. She looked at me with big blue eyes and timidly asked, "Can I see your baby mule?"

I winced. "We'll see. Maybe after dinner." I took her cowboy hat and settled it down on her head and said, "Now scoot."

Wind Dancer had been the hit of the guest ranch where I worked. Everyone had wanted to pet the baby—all the time—for the last couple of months. At first I loved showing off my little mule, but as the demands became overwhelming, I limited the visits to after dinner. Then, a couple days ago, I was in an accident and severely burned both my feet with a pan full of boiling grease. A large blister covered each foot. I wrapped and tucked them into a pair of oversized water shoes.

I balanced the dishes and slowly and painfully shuffled to the kitchen. *I'm tired of the baby thing, and I've got so much work to do. Besides, I just want to lie down and put up my feet. Why do I feel guilty?* Then I remembered horse-crazy me at Sarah's age.

Just before sunset, I met Sarah and her mom at the pasture. I showed Sarah all of Wind Dancer's favorite spots to get scratched. When Wind Dancer expressed her gratitude by scrunching up her face and curling her lips, Sarah burst out laughing, and I forgot about my feet. Every night for the rest of the week, we met in the pasture.

When we said our good-byes, Sarah's mom said, "Your mule was the highlight of our whole vacation. Sarah will cherish these memories forever."

I want that kind of crazy, happy joy, God.... Yes, other-worldly joy like that. The kind you could search the world over—and find only in a child.

ANN VOSKAMP

He will yet fill your mouth with laughter and your lips with shouts of joy.

JOB 8:21

Wholehearted, ready laughter heals, encourages, relaxes anyone within hearing distance. The laughter that springs from love makes wide the space around it—gives room for the loved one to enter in. Real laughter welcomes and never shuts out.

EUGENIA PRICE

He made you so you could share in His creation, could love and laugh and know Him.

TED GRIFFEN

*I*t's not always easy to laugh when we feel like crying. Motherhood is as difficult at times as it is joyful. We often let the weight of our responsibilities stifle the joy within us. But when we pause for even a moment to look into the face of our smiling child, joy bubbles to the surface. Smiles emerge. Worries fall to the wayside, and what's important becomes clear. God made us for each other, and when we laugh together our spirits rejoice. Laughter comes from a place of joy—a deep-down, God-dwelling, light-filled place. If it fills our days, it will feed our souls, and our children will be healthier and happier because of it.

BONNIE JENSEN

Life, love,
and laughter—
what priceless gifts
to give our children.

PHYLLIS CAMPBELL DRYDEN

It is often just as sacred to
laugh as it is to pray.

CHARLES R. SWINDOLL

She is clothed with strength
and dignity;
she can laugh at the days
to come.

PROVERBS 31:25

I meant to do my work today
But a brown bird sang in the apple tree,
And a butterfly flitted across the field,
And all the leaves were calling me.
And the wind went sighing over the land,
Tossing the grasses to and fro,
And a rainbow held out his shining hand—
So what could I do but laugh and go?

RICHARD LEGALLIENNE

May the righteous be glad and rejoice before God; may they be happy
and joyful. Sing to God, sing in praise of his name, extol him who rides
on the clouds; rejoice before him—his name is the LORD.

PSALM 68:3-4

When children's eyes are smiling
'Tis God's love that's shining through
With glints of joy and laughter
What good medicine for you!

MARGARET FISHBACK POWERS

The Work of Laughter

BY MARY BROWN

*There is nothing better for people than to be happy
and to do good while they live. That each of them may...find satisfaction
in all their toil—this is the gift of God.*

ECCLESIASTES 3:12–13

I drove to church a bit reluctantly this evening, weary after making dinner and teaching my last piano lesson. It had been a long day, and I was starting to resent last Sunday's request by our pastor's wife that we give the church kitchen a thorough cleaning before our upcoming festival.

As I entered the social hall, I saw the same few people who seem always to help out. I dipped a rag into a bucket of pine-scented cleaner and started scrubbing down the hood over the large stove, trying to remove the accumulation of grease. Next to me, James Erickson and his son Jimmy were washing walls. They were laughing and joking, teasing each other about who was getting his part cleaner and purposely dripping water on each other.

Their humor was contagious. Soon I was laughing along and scrubbing more vigorously. We joked with Jimmy about how we wished we had his teenage energy. "Isn't it hard to work with us old folks?"

Laughing, he said, "Well, actually, I'm having a lot more fun than I thought I would!"

James put his arm around his son's shoulder and said, "Always remember, son, there's special grace given to you when you work for the church."

As I wrung out my rag, I pondered James's words. Here I'd been complaining about the needs in our parish and the heavy workload for a few. My attitude needed the good scrubbing it got from James and Jimmy that night!

Take time to laugh; it is the music of the soul.

Teach me, Father, to value each day,
to live, to love, to laugh, to play.
KATHI MILLS

Rejoice always, pray without ceasing,
in everything give thanks; for this is the will of God.
1 THESSALONIANS 5:16–18 NKJV

If you can learn to laugh in spite of the circumstances
that surround you, you will enrich others,
enrich yourself, and more than that, you will last!
BARBARA JOHNSON

Let me run loose and free, celebrating GOD's great work,
Every bone in my body laughing, singing, "GOD, there's no one like you."

PSALM 35:9 MSG

Joy is more than my spontaneous expression of laughter, gaiety, and lightness. It is deeper than an emotional expression of happiness. Joy is a growing, evolving manifestation of God in my life as I walk with Him.

BONNIE MONSON

I will rejoice in the LORD,
I will be joyful in God my Savior.

HABAKKUK 3:18

A good laugh is sunshine in a house.

WILLIAM MAKEPEACE THACKERAY

The wind rushing through the grass, the thrush in the treetops, and children tumbling in senseless mirth stir in us a bright faith in life.

DONALD CULROSS PEATTIE

CHAPTER 10

The simple joy of Faith

If it can be verified, we don't need faith.... Faith is for that which lies
on the other side of reason. Faith is what makes life bearable,
with all its tragedies and ambiguities and sudden, startling joys.

MADELEINE L'ENGLE

We work with you for your joy,
because it is by faith that you stand firm.

2 CORINTHIANS 1:24

A Foundation of Faith

BY BONNIE JENSEN

This trust in God, this faith, is the firm foundation under everything that makes life worth living. It's our handle on what we can't see.

HEBREWS 11:1 MSG

If we are constantly awaiting the magnificent,
we will miss the miracles in the moment.

My sister recalls a simple craving for orange juice. She had big, soul cravings at the time—food to fill her empty cupboards and feed her three children; a way to cover the shut-off notice glaring at her from the tabletop; relief from the weight of so many physical needs slumping her shoulders but having little effect on her contagious smile. A spirit so bright finds an exit point from the body. Her eyes were not dimmed, and her mouth refused to frown.

There were those around her who knew of her needs, and one who answered when God tapped on the door of her heart. She opened wide and filled my sister's front porch with bags of groceries during the church service that Sunday morning. How could she have known that while she was doing that, my sister was praying…telling God how good a cold glass of orange juice would taste. Among her countless needs, a small desire whispered.

Tears fell on the porch steps when my sister saw the gallon of freshly squeezed orange juice, clearly visible from a bag of generosity and answered prayer. She daily held the promise that her needs would be met—but in a smaller act, the Father revealed His love for a daughter in a way that made a deep and lasting impression on her heart and the hearts of her children.

These are the moments we can't afford to miss. The heart-seeking moments that defy questions, cancel doubts, and defeat fear. The ways God shows His faithfulness in breathtaking, personal exchanges. I *see* you—I *know* you—I *hear* you.

Nothing on this earth can stop His love from reaching us when we need to see and feel it most…and thankfully, nothing will keep Him from showing it.

Just as angels are attracted to the light of joy and kindness,
so too, are miracles attracted to the lamp of faith and love.

MARY AUGUSTINE

Whenever you face trials of any kind, consider it nothing but joy,
because you know that the testing of your faith produces endurance;
and let endurance have its full effect, so that you may be mature
and complete, lacking in nothing.

JAMES 1:2–4 NRSV

Framed Faith

BY MARY ANN O'ROARK

Wisdom is with the aged, and understanding in length of days.

JOB 12:12 RSV

*F*inally, I was cleaning out the back—way back—of my bedroom closet. I pulled out a flattened tennis shoe (only one—why on earth had I kept it?), a bag of yarn I'd used years ago for needlepoint, a clump of yellowing drycleaner bags. As dust filtered through the air, I was already ready to quit. But there was one more item, something flat, along the wall.

I pulled it out—a framed picture. I wiped off the dust with a crumpled sock. It was a picture I remembered seeing as a little girl in my grandmother Paisley's house in Steubenville, Ohio. Later, my mother had kept it in our home, displayed in an upstairs bedroom. It was a picture of Jesus on His knees in a garden, gazing upward in prayer. As a child and teenager, I'd loved it; as a cynical adult, I'd rolled my eyes and dismissed it as sentimental and irrelevant.

Had my grandmother cared enough to cut this from the pages of a book or magazine and put it in a frame? I pushed open the tabs at the back of the frame and pulled out the cardboard. Yes, that's what it was—an illustration or reproduction, probably from some kind of Easter devotional book. On the back, I read this blurb in flowing type: "The risen Christ brought inspiration, joy, and cheer to His disciples. To all who follow Him in simple faith, He does the same today."

Tears stung my eyes. In an instant, all intellectual fussiness and self-important judgment was gone, the purity and profundity in this simple statement rang true across the ages. An iconic picture cut out and framed by my beloved grandmother probably seventy-five years ago now glowed with astonishing new life.

I copied the words, reassembled the picture in its frame, pasted the words on the back of the frame, and recorded them in my journal—and in my heart.

I will give thanks to you, LORD,
with all my heart;
I will tell of all your
wonderful deeds.
I will be glad and
rejoice in you;
I will sing the praises of
your name, O Most High.

PSALM 9:1–2

If our children have the background of a godly, happy home and this unshakable faith that the Bible is indeed the Word of God, they will have a foundation that the forces of hell cannot shake.

RUTH BELL GRAHAM

THE IMPORTANCE OF CHURCH

Research shows that children who go to church once a week have lower percentages of teen pregnancies, higher GPAs, drop out less, live longer, and are generally better behaved and more well-adjusted. So how do you go about getting your child excited about church?

1. Attend church services yourself and talk about the good experiences and friends you have there.
2. Pray daily with your kids, including prayers for church and other churchgoers.
3. Encourage their father to go to church regularly. Research shows that factor has more influence on a child's church attendance than any other.
4. Be sensitive to the amount of age-appropriate activities offered. Volunteer to lead more if there aren't enough for your child's age.
5. Make the trip to and from church as fun and hassle-free as possible.
6. Bring church home with you, repeating lessons learned, dancing to worship songs with your children, reading the Bible verses from the sermon as a family.

Lord...give me the gift of faith to be renewed and shared
with others each day. Teach me to live this moment only,
looking neither to the past with regret, nor the future with apprehension.
Let love be my aim and my life a prayer.

ROSEANN ALEXANDER-ISHAM

Let us hold unswervingly to the hope we profess,
for he who promised is faithful. And let us consider how we may spur
one another on toward love and good deeds.

HEBREWS 10:23–24

If one is joyful, it means that one is faithfully living for God and that
nothing else counts; and if one gives joy to others, one is doing God's
work. With joy without and joy within, all is well.

JANET ERSKINE STUART

*The first and finest lesson that parents
can teach their children is faith and courage.*

SMILEY BLANTON

Developing Faith

BY PAM KIDD

Gray hair is a crown of glory.
PROVERBS 16:31 NLT

*S*ometime back, I read an article on why hair turns gray: It is related to the body's production of something called melanocyte. But experience tells me that gray hair is mostly caused by children. Not other people's children, but your own.

Actually, my first gray hair and our son Brock's first step were a simultaneous occurrence. That exact moment also represents a milestone in my faith walk. That's when my prayer-life began in earnest.

Keri, our daughter, on the other hand, didn't contribute much to the "snow on the mountain" until she decided it was time to be a teenager. Less dramatic but just as heart-stopping, her antics came in spurts, always with the same effect on her mother's tresses: Phone rings. "Hello." "Mama, let me speak to Dad. Now!" Or worse: Phone rings. "Hello." "Mrs. Kidd"—Keri's boyfriend's voice—"let me speak to Dr. Kidd. Now!"

As mothers, we certainly don't want our children to be afraid. We want them to develop confidence, to believe in themselves. So we pray and we gray and we look forward. Which brings me to my final point: What grays my hair builds my faith. I guess that's why a wise man once said: "Gray hair is a crown of glory."

Finding acceptance with joy, whatever the circumstances of life—
whether they are petty annoyances or fiery trials—
this is a living faith that grows.

MARY LOU STEIGLEDER

Every part of Scripture is God-breathed and useful one way or another—
showing us truth, exposing our rebellion, correcting our mistakes,
training us to live God's way. Through the Word we are put together
and shaped up for the tasks God has for us.

2 TIMOTHY 3:16–17 MSG

Sometimes remembering the day of our salvation
or remembering answered prayer is the last knot on the end
of our rope to cling to. When we're struggling with doubts,
looking back at the foundation of our faith is a positive activity.

VIRGINIA THOMAS

*Trust in the LORD with all your heart
and do not lean on your own understanding.
In all your ways acknowledge Him,
and He will make your paths straight.*

PROVERBS 3:5–6 NASB

I think of faith as a kind of whistling in the dark because,
in much the same way, it helps to give us courage and to hold the
shadows at bay. To whistle in the dark...demonstrate[s],
if only to ourselves, that not even the dark can quite overcome
our trust in the ultimate triumph of the Living Light.

FREDERICK BUECHNER

God is as near as a whispered prayer
No matter the time or place,
Whether skies are blue
And all's right with you,
Or clouds dim the road you face.
In His mercy and great compassion
He will ease, He will help, He will share!
Whatever your lot,
Take heart in the thought:
God's as near as a whispered prayer!

JON GILBERT

The fundamental fact of existence is that this trust in God,
this faith, is the firm foundation under everything
that makes life worth living. It's our handle on what we can't see.

HEBREWS 11:1 MSG

CHICKEN SALAD FINGER SANDWICHES

Whether you are having a Bible study with your kids, your girlfriends, or your family, these sandwiches are great to have on hand. Pair them with a steaming pot of tea or sparkling fresh lemonade.

Ingredients

- 2 oven-roasted or rotisserie chicken breasts, roughly chopped
- ½ cup mayonnaise
- 2 teaspoons lemon juice
- ⅓ cup chopped fresh herbs (dill, parsley, basil, chives, or whatever is available)
- salt and freshly cracked black pepper
- 8 slices thin white bread, crust removed

Directions

Combine the chicken, mayonnaise, lemon juice, mixed herbs, salt, and pepper. Spoon the mixture over half the bread slices then top with the remaining slices.

Slice each sandwich into thirds to make three fingers or use cookie cutters to cut them into fun shapes. Serve immediately or cover and refrigerate until ready to serve.

God, help me to be honest so my children
will learn honesty.
Help me to be kind so my children
will learn kindness.
Help me to be faithful so my children
will learn faith.
Help me to love so that my children
will be loving.

MARIAN WRIGHT EDELMAN

ACKNOWLEDGMENTS

Special thanks to Bonnie Jensen for writing the chapter introductions and other pieces for *The Simple Joys of Motherhood*.

"Talking Together" by Julie Garmon is reprinted with permission from *Guideposts* magazine. Copyright © 2008 by Guideposts. All rights reserved. "Stitched Together" by Kathy Morrison is reprinted with permission from *Guideposts* magazine. Copyright © 2009 by Guideposts. All rights reserved. "A Togetherness Table" by Carol Kuykendall is reprinted with permission from *Daily Guideposts*. Copyright © 2005 by Guideposts. All rights reserved. "Bound Together" by Brigitte Weeks is reprinted with permission from *Daily Guideposts*. Copyright © 2009 by Guideposts. All rights reserved. "Words to Grow On" by Dee Wallace Stone is reprinted with permission from *Guideposts* M\magazine. Copyright © 1990 by Guideposts. All rights reserved. "The Sweetest Words" by Erin Keeley Marshall is reprinted with permission from *Mornings with Jesus*. Copyright © 2011 by Guideposts. All rights reserved. "Pray Always" by Pattie Phillips is reprinted with permission from *Daily Guideposts*. Copyright © 1981 by Guideposts. All rights reserved. "A Birthday Wish" by Karen Barnett is reprinted with permission from *Guideposts* magazine. Copyright © 2010 by Guideposts. All rights reserved. "Remember to Celebrate" by Julie Garmon is reprinted with permission from *Daily Guideposts*. Copyright © 2009 by Guideposts. All rights reserved. "A Reason to Party" by Mary Lou Carney is reprinted with permission from *Daily Guideposts*. Copyright © 2010 by Guideposts. All rights reserved. "Give Expectantly" by Roberta Messner is reprinted with permission from *Daily Guideposts*. Copyright © 2010 by Guideposts. All rights reserved. "The Joy of Fireflies" by Sabra Ciancanelli is reprinted with permission from *Daily Guideposts*. Copyright © 2006 by Guideposts. All rights reserved. "A Present for My Mother" by Keith Miller is reprinted with permission from *Daily Guideposts*. Copyright © 2010 by Guideposts. All rights reserved. "Glued Together" by Mary Brown is reprinted with permission from *Daily Guideposts*. Copyright © 2001 by Guideposts. All rights reserved. "Full of Love" by Roberta Rogers is reprinted with permission from *Daily*

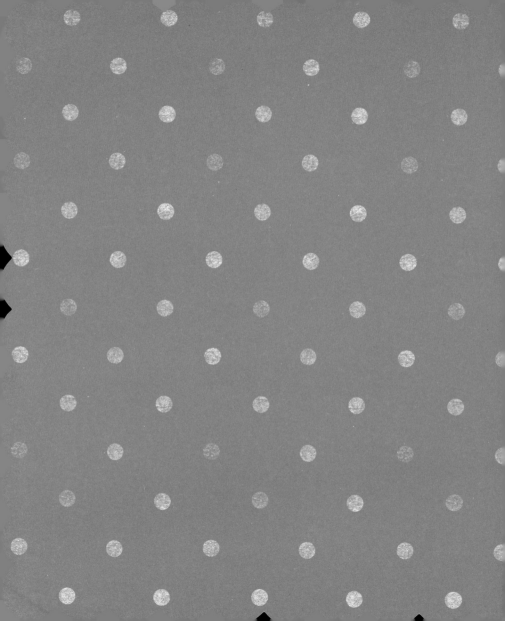